WITHDRAWN
C0-AZE-421
3 1205 00058 1
DANVILLE PUBLIC LIBRARY

The Ziegfeld Follies

THE ZIEGFELD FOLLIES

MARJORIE FARNSWORTH

with an introduction by Billie Burke Ziegfeld

Bonanza Books · New York

Acknowledgments

I wish to express my appreciation for the help and encouragement in the preparation of this book received from William Randolph Hearst, Jr., Editor-in-Chief of the Hearst Newspapers; Louis Sobol, columnist of New York *Journal-American* and King Features Syndicate; The Ziegfeld Club and in particular Kathryn Dix, who was secretary to Ziegfeld; International News Photos and in particular Ed. J. Martin for his research in its extensive library; Virginia Carrick, Constance Campbell and Peter Van Doren, editors of G. P. Putnam's Sons; the staff of the New York *Journal-American* Reference Library, and the New York Public Library.

MARJORIE FARNSWORTH

This edition is published by Bonanza Books, a division of Crown Publishers, Inc., by arrangement with G. P. Putnam's Sons.

Library of Congress Catalog Card Number: 56-10227

Manufactured in the United States of America

TO

Millicent de Freytas Farnsworth

Foreword

by Billie Burke Ziegfeld

Miss Farnsworth's entertaining text for this book and all the wonderful pictures tell the stories of so many beautiful and talented people that I feel quite shy about writing a Foreword, especially as I never had any direct connection with the Ziegfeld Follies myself. I never appeared in a Follies, and never had any part in the management, but heaven knows I heard enough about them each year. I used to share the excitement — and the worries — as the June opening approached and my husband became more and more engrossed in his new show. What a lot of fun it all was — and what a terrific lot of work, too!

That is the only thing this book does not, perhaps, reflect completely. It all seemed then — and still does — very glamorous and easy to take, but the writers and directors and musicians and backstage people all had to be on the alert for weeks and months before and after the Follies and the other big Ziegfeld shows were given to the public. You didn't see them but they were there.

In my own little book I have told how the rising costs of these shows gradually made it more and more difficult to produce them. My husband couldn't and wouldn't spare expense on the settings and costumes, and he paid his stars and the girls themselves very high salaries. He delighted in finding new designers and composers, men like Joseph Urban, Ben Ali Haggin, and James Reynolds, or Berlin and Gershwin, and he simply couldn't stop being more and more lavish with every show. In the end they were costing hundreds of thousands of dollars and often it took years to pay off the initial investment. The result was personal tragedy for their creator, but

JOHN ALFRED PIVER

Billie Burke

the world remembers Mr. Ziegfeld as the man who revealed a whole new world of color and light and gaiety in the modern musical revue.

Anna Held (who gave Mr. Ziegfeld the idea of the Follies), lovely Lillian Lorraine, Marilyn Miller (the *Sally* one, of course), Dolores — how many romantic memories these names bring up! And the men — Will Rogers, Mr. Fields, Bert Williams, Leon Errol — they cheered the distracted and jittery twenties as no others did.

So I am glad to see this tribute, and to note that Miss Farnsworth dispels the legend that the average Ziegfeld girl was merely a featherbrained, pretty creature with no real gifts for the theatre — a sort of doll who had just enough intelligence to walk on and off stage without falling flat on her charming posterior. I must confess that I feel a great deal of sympathy for these lovelies, having been typed for so long by Hollywood as a bird-witted lady myself.

It's true, of course, that quite a few of them had their troubles, marital and otherwise, and that not many ever became distinguished scientists like Justine Johnstone; or witty stars like Ina Claire, or great ladies of Hollywood like Irene Dunne, but I'd be willing to wager that most of them could hold their own in any reasonably intelligent gathering — and I doubt if that can be said of today's hipsters and unholy "rock-and-rollers." (I believe they call them that, don't they?)

The proof, I think, is in the Ziegfeld Club, the group that meets in New York every so often to recall the good old days of the Follies and the Midnight Frolics, and of *Show Boat* and *Kid Boots* and so on. They are as fine and as charming a lot of women as you'd be able to bring together as alumnae from any other institution of learning, and I have always been proud to be associated with them in their annual balls and charity work.

They have given the author of this book valuable information and support, and so have many old collaborators and friends of my husband. Through them it has become one of the really authentic records of a fabulous man and his era. I hope a great many people, old and young, will enjoy it.

chapter one

Florenz Ziegfeld was the leading entrepreneur of sensual desire, desire in chiffon and lace you might call it; and the bailiff of glorification of the Americal girl and himself, in a fabulous era which seemed to those who lived in it the utmost of sophistication, and which seems to us now both Byzantine and naïve.

The quality of the age was magnified, as in a huge mirror bordered with rosebuds, in the Ziegfeld Follies from 1907 to 1931. Women could not possibly be as desirable, beautiful and breath-taking as that . . . yet they were, under the Ziegfeld master touch of illusion. How many he glorified — Anna Held, Billie Burke, Ina Claire, Mae Murray, Marilyn Miller, Billie Dove, Lillian Lorraine, Olive Thomas, up to some three thousand of them over the years, in the Follies and out!

What was this touch? What were the components of this illusion that brought millionaires night after night to see the same Follies over and over, that induced Diamond Jim Brady to pay $750 for ten opening night seats, that brought to the girls gifts of previous jewels tucked in bouquets of long-stemmed backstage roses?

First, Ziegfeld knew the subtle line between desire and lust, between good taste and vulgarity, and never crossed it. He came close a few times but he never quite crossed it. Second, the exhibitionism which was part of his private life was not contrived. It was an integral part of him, part of the personality mechanism that made him what he was: a gambler who had an almost childish irresponsibility toward the value of money and an equally childish conviction that he could always get some more when he wanted it. Most of the time he was astonishingly right. And finally, he had a sense of showmanship and of female beauty that was the despair of his competitors.

There are innumerable instances that attest to his character:

In January of 1906 Ziegfeld went to Europe for a holiday. In Monte Carlo he won a million and a half francs at the gambling tables. With his winnings he lived in true Ziegfeldian style and even started a racing stable. Four months later with a couple of francs left after he had paid his passage, he returned home, flat broke and undisturbed.

INTERNATIONAL NEWS PHOTOS, INC.

Mother of Florenz Ziegfeld

INTERNATIONAL NEWS PHOTOS, INC.

Florenz Ziegfeld with his brothers and sisters.

Sending telegrams up to a thousand words in length was one of his costliest eccentricities. He enjoyed dictating them almost as much as he liked seeing his name in the papers. As one Broadway wag remarked: "If Ziegfeld dies, sell Western Union short."

He lived in what has become known as the golden era and he was happiest surrounding himself with all that was colorful and representative of the times. He had three golden telephones on his desk and enjoyed giving little bags full of coins — often twenty-dollar gold pieces — to friends, girls or people he ran into when these gleam-of-gold moments overcame him. But one of his prized possessions was a French telephone he brought back from Paris at considerable cost, which remained on his desk until his death.

He traveled across the United States in private railroad cars always carrying his own chef. It was rumored at the time that he had one cook just to prepare his liver and bacon alone. On the other hand he had so marked an aversion to personal luggage that he often packed his toilet articles in a newspaper. It appears to have been a genuine idiosyncrasy, for Ziegfeld above all else admired elegance.

The fact that his bank balance and credit weren't always liquid didn't change his way of life. A wealthy friend who had advanced thousands to him got a wire from California where Ziegfeld had been sojourning which read:

> WITH THOROUGH APPRECIATION FOR THE PRODIGAL KINDNESSES FOR WHICH I AM INDEBTED TO YOU, I MUST IMPLORE YOU TO EXTEND TO ME YOUR GENEROUS HELP. THIS IS A LIFE-AND-DEATH MATTER. I NEED $25,000 AND I NEED IT IMMEDIATELY. COULD YOU FIND IT IN YOUR HEART TO TELEGRAPH IT TO ME?

The friend did and Ziegfeld used it to return to New York by private car. It wasn't exactly life-and-death but it was vital to his ego.

There is little question that he had affairs with some of his glorified girls. Billie Burke, in her charmingly candid account of her marriage to Ziegfeld, tells of his coming home one morning at five o'clock "after seeing Olive Thomas, I suppose?" She seized a silver soup ladle and whacked him on the shoulders with it. He laughed and carried her upstairs. Another time he said, "The trouble with you, Billie, is you always pick the wrong girl."

Whatever the extent of his extramarital excursions and however violent the scenes with his wives, Anna Held and Billie Burke, Ziegfeld seemed always able to hold their sub-surface affection. There was only one girl who caused Billie Burke deep and desperate fear. Her name was Marilyn Miller.

A final facet of the Magnificent Ziegfeld's character is that he could be and often was extravagantly generous and tender. Thus he usually treated his wives, and he was infinitely so always to his beloved daughter, Patricia.

There is little in his early years to indicate the man Ziegfeld was to be. He was born March 21, 1868, into a solid, comfortable, middle-class German family in Chicago. His father, Dr. Florenz Ziegfeld, sometimes called Colonel, was a musical impresario with a solid but undistinguished knowledge of music. He brought Johann Strauss to this country in 1872 and managed his appearances. The elder Ziegfeld founded the Chicago Musical College, still extant, which at first was located in the parlor of the Ziegfeld home. Later he assisted Theodore Thomas in organizing the Chicago Symphony.

The boy Ziegfeld was anemic, frail, apathetic and often ill. He studied music lethargically and under parental compulsion. He had no zest for it, no interest in anything, and he seemed to have about as much vitality and imagination as overcooked spinach. When he was seventeen his parents, more in desperation than hope, sent him to a Wyoming cattle ranch.

When, after several months of getting acquainted with cowboys, horses and six-shooters, the young Ziegfeld returned home, he was amazingly transformed. He was energetic, healthy and cheerful. He also began to show a will of his own. He refused his father's suggestion that he should learn his business, though he consented to do clerical work in the Musical College. But he was merely treading water. He did not have to tread very long, for Buffalo Bill and his Wild West show came into Chicago one spring morning.

That night an awed audience watched Buffalo Bill as he demonstrated his marksmanship, finishing with a fancy hand-twirl of his gun, nonchalantly stroking his yellow goatee with the other. "Any takers?" he asked of his admiring audience. There was only one, a gangling youth who climbed up on the platform to the accompaniment of good-natured jeers and catcalls. He didn't quite equal the master's marksmanship but when the smoke cleared away, Buffalo Bill said, "Want a job, kid?" When the circus pulled up stakes there was a new name added to the payroll.

Two weeks later a florid-faced, heavy-set man caught up with the show in one of the small towns outside Chicago. He displayed little interest in the performance until a young man dressed in buckskins came on stage with a pair of six-shooters and began hitting bull's-eyes with an air of indifferent aplomb. When the act was finished and the youth, the applause still ringing in his ears, was walking back to his dressing tent the older man caught up with him.

"Florenz!" he shouted, grabbing him by the fringe on his jacket.

"Aw — Pop." The youth paled under his theatrical coat of tan.

"Get off those crazy things. Mama is waiting for you."

On the train home young Florenz, his dreams gone with the smoke from his guns, was told authoritatively: "It is a bad business, this show business, Florenz. Better you should stay home and I will make you business manager of the college."

And to his father that seemed the end of all the "bad business" that was later to make his son one of the greatest showmen the world has known.

Where does coincidence end and destiny take over? This can be a teasing question in the nights when sleep eludes you, but it is probable that it never entered Ziegfeld's head to reflect upon it. He had had his taste of showmanship. He had savored it and found it good and now he was waiting for another opportunity. It was not long coming, for his father received the assignment to provide the musical entertainment for the Chicago World's Fair. The elder Ziegfeld set ploddingly about the task, then suddenly found, to his surprise or chagrin, or perhaps both, that his son had wildly extravagant ideas that would not be denied.

The young Ziegfeld took off for Europe, recklessly spent the exposition committee's money, and returned with seven military bands and an awesome collection of French and Russian performers. Alas, they were a flop. They did not care for Chicago, nor Chicago for them. A lesser egotist might have been crushed, but Ziegfeld, even at this early age, was showing the signs of an overwhelming, invulnerable confidence. Today, it might have led him by force to a psychiatrist's couch with consequent loss to the community of his talent for the glorification of female splendor — and who will say that would not have been a catastrophe?

At any rate he was introduced presently to the world's strong man, Eugene Sandow, that mighty hulk of muscle and sinew whose torso haunted female dreams (it was a naïve age, remember) and whose back resembled the ripples in a washboard. Sandow demanded $1,000 a week, a monstrous amount in those days. Ziegfeld persuaded him to accept ten per cent of the receipts. As result, Sandow found himself making an unbelievable $3,000 a week. Ziegfeld really put him over. He spent his last $5,000 in exploitation, and he lured in the crowds to gasp as the strong man bent iron bars like hairpins and won a tug of war against four horses — or so it seemed.

But the supreme touch of the maestro was yet to come. By an incredible feat of persuasion Ziegfeld induced some of the most respected dowagers of their time, like Mrs. Potter Palmer, irreproachably entrenched within the battlements of social splendor and wealth, to journey backstage to feel Sandow's mountainous muscles. How Ziegfeld plotted this coup and carried it off remains one of the darker mysteries. He contrived also that the "ohs" and "ahs" of the dowagers, as their fingers marveled at such brutish male strength, could be heard considerably farther than backstage. He established

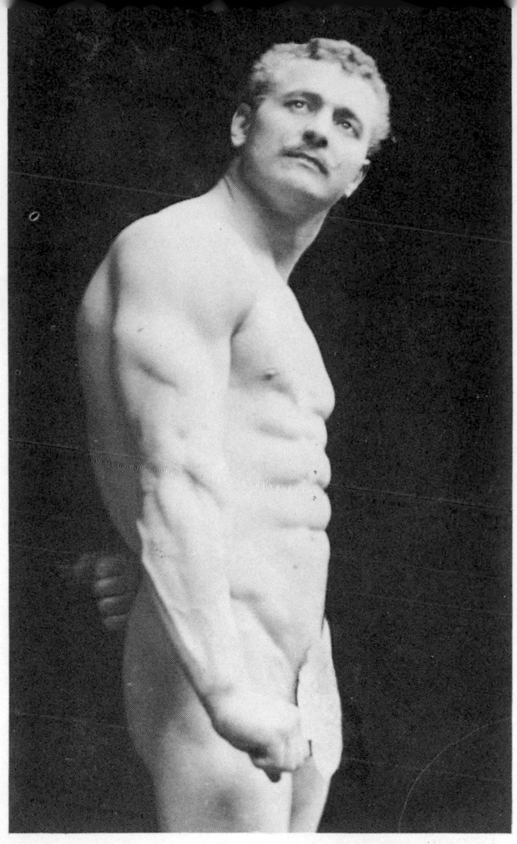

THE ZIEGFELD CLUB

The Great Sandow

Ziegfeld with Sandow in Sacramento in 1888.

THE ZIEGFELD CLUB

INTERNATIONAL NEWS PHOTOS, INC.

Ziegfeld in 1890

a precedent, one of those brief, flashing and compulsive whims of society, and thereafter men and women of prominence felt themselves bound to make the backstage visit. You were no one, really no one, my dear, unless you had felt Sandow's muscles.

Having found a good thing, Ziegfeld exploited Sandow to the limit — and beyond. He toured the country with him and, when the strong man's feats of strength began to pall, he arranged in San Francisco to have Sandow battle with what was billed as a man-eating lion. Ziegfeld let it be known this was to be more savage and elemental than anything ancient Rome had conceived. San Francisco was aghast, agape and gasping for gore. The tickets sold for staggering prices. Came the evening and came also the disillusionment. The man-eating lion was coquettish and bored and Sandow was reluctantly fierce. So that was the real end of the Sandow adventure.

After a rather embarrassing interlude with an act called the Dancing Ducks of Denmark, which was short-lived and a slipshod error on the part of the master, Ziegfeld arrived in New York. There he met Lew Weber, of Weber and Fields. The partners had fallen out and Ziegfeld entered into an agreement with Weber to put on a spectacle at Weber's Music Hall. It did pretty well, until, in turn, Ziegfeld and Weber disagreed, a mild way of saying they found themselves cemented in mutual hostility.

Ziegfeld sold out his interest and departed for the playgrounds of Europe. And that was how he happened to meet Anna Held, the girl who sang "Won't You Come and Play Wiz Me?" And that was how he came to love, after his fashion, and marry and glorify Anna Held. Their meeting is as shrouded in the mists of the past as Anna's birth. Did they meet in a Paris music hall where Ziegfeld, quite by chance, wandered in and heard her singing her repertoire of popular French and German songs? Or was it, as some cautious historians have indicated, in London? The answer seems to have died with Anna and Ziegfeld, as did the question of Anna's parentage. She was born either in Warsaw, the daughter of Polish Jews, or in Paris of French parentage — you can take your choice. And there is a wispy, tantalizing rumor that actually her birthplace was Indiana. Obviously, for reasons best known to her, Anna didn't bother to set the record straight. She was what she wanted to be — billed as a Parisian music-hall singer and a minor toast of the Continent.

Actually Anna was not a striking beauty. She had a plump little figure laced in at the waist until her hips jutted out horizontally. Her hand-spanned eighteen-inch waist was later to become the envy of the ladies in the audience, but it was her eyes, mischievous and with a trace of naughtiness, that delighted the men. She was a tiny girl, a little over five feet in height, with a halo of light brown hair and a nose a little too long to agree with an artist's ideal. To Americans she was the epitome of Gallic spice and naughtiness.

Ziegfeld at a rehearsal of the Follies.

THE ZIEGFELD CLUB

But Ziegfeld had already started glorifying her before Anna stepped onto the pier and into her first American press reception. Anna was dressed in a white silk dress dotted with pink figures. Now and then in moving about in her gay little fashion, she disclosed the edge of a garnet silk petticoat trimmed with black lace. Her stockings were black and her tiny feet were encased in black satin slippers. Her right hand was decorated with diamond and sapphire rings, bracelets of the same jewels went almost up to the elbow of her right arm, and around her throat was a brooch of diamonds interwoven to form her initials.

Ziegfeld himself had gone down to Quarantine in a yacht with a party of friends to welcome his wasp-waisted bewitcher and personally escorted her to the flower-filled suite at the Hotel Savoy where she held an informal reception throughout the day. There she tirelessly and graciously explained her penchants and dislikes about everything pertaining to Anna Held.

Such as:

Bloomers when bicycling? Much, much too shocking. Besides, Anna hadn't brought her bicycle over although she would get one if it wasn't too expensive. This was accompanied by merry peals of laughter. London's

Ziegfeld with the *Show Boat* Company. Ziegfeld, Howard Marsh, Eva Puck and Norma Terris; Charles Winninger and Sammy White

THE ZIEGFELD CLUB

PICTURE COLLECTION, NEW YORK PUBLIC LIBRARY

Ziegfeld with Eddie Cantor in the 20's.

Trafalgar Square Cycling Club had given her one — along with an ornate diamond necklace — and she could always have that sent over. Naturally, she adored London. She had cried most of the time on the boat and suffered a touch of *mal-de-mer* and was sorry the whole way across that she had ever left Paris.

Yes indeed Anna answered all her questioners, running emotionally through the Held repertoire to the delight of Ziegfeld, who hovered in the background and watched with a smile that grew broader and broader as the hours went on.

A few days later Anna made her first American appearance at the Herald Square Theatre. Her songs were fashioned after those of Yvette Guilbert and included such dear-to-that-age songs as *"Maman, Achète-Moi Ça," "Faut des Femmes," "En Suivant,"* and always ended with her famous "Come Play Wiz Me." She didn't dance but her gestures were graceful and provocative, and the theatre was filled. But this was just a warm-up for her opening in the play *A Parlor Match,* for which Ziegfeld was paying her $1,500 a week under a three-month contract. The showman in Ziegfeld had realized that the little singer needed first of all a debut in a field where she had confidence, before he launched her on Broadway as an actress. He proved with his usual what-an-audience-wants intuition to be right. From the night *A*

THE ZIEGFELD CLUB

Florenz Ziegfeld in his office at the Ziegfeld Theatre — 1930

INTERNATIONAL NEWS PHOTOS, INC.

Ziegfeld at a Palm Beach Ball — 1929

Parlor Match opened, Anna and Ziegfeld were walking the path that was to lead them to fame and fortune together for fourteen years.

With Ziegfeld's genius directing her, Anna made bigger and better headlines. This is not to suggest that Anna wasn't able to take care of herself. On the contrary she was an extremely shrewd young woman and when it came to personal considerations of money she was even more shrewd than Ziegfeld himself. Anna was a willing and accomplished conspirator in the craft of exploitation.

Her milk baths became the talk of New York and of the world wherever papers were read. In an inspired moment Ziegfeld ordered gallons of milk to be delivered for Anna's daily bath. The papers were lukewarm for a while when he announced the little French star kept her body beautiful and her complexion perfection by dunking herself every morning in a liquid that up until then had been considered something to drink. Then, undaunted by the lack of newspaper space — the milk-bath routine was dying of inattention — Ziegfeld poured into it the brandy of a lawsuit against himself. He had the milkman sue him, and that did it. Anna's baths were famous and sales of milk zoomed. Women everywhere, at least those with any daring and money, were sitting up to their necks in tubs of milk. And Ziegfeld soon escorted a group of skeptical reporters to Anna's suite and showed her immersed in the sticky liquid. *N'est-ce pas,* Anna asked, how else could she keep her satinlike skin?

The automobile-racing fad was sweeping America at this time and Anna, with little urging from Ziegfeld, proposed that American women take it up. She issued a challenge, through the newspapers naturally, for any American woman to meet her in a road race from New York City to Philadelphia — a distance of one hundred miles. While in Paris that past summer Anna had tooled her four-in-hand dexterously along the country roads until, bored with that, she transferred her affection and fancy to automobiles. She imposed one condition in her challenge and that was the American woman was to drive an American car and Anna a French one. And she announced as a warning to anyone who was daring enough to pick up the challenge that she held a couple of speed records. This was more of the Ziegfeld genius in all probability, but nevertheless Anna proudly announced that she had driven ninety miles in 193 minutes, and, as further proof of her daring and driving skill, once covered three and one half miles in five minutes.

Whether it was Ziegfeld or Anna who had a sense of the dramatic in her clothes no one will ever know, but they were the talk of the time. When she played in *Papa's Wife,* one critic, in describing the opening night, wrote that "Miss Held weeps, sleeps and walks in real lace." Her costumes cost $40,000 in that elegant bit of nonsense and Ziegfeld paid $20,000 for one gown, famous as the poppy dress. It was a yellow crepe de Chine, trimmed with poppies in full bloom and with falling petals ranging from the palest shade to the deepest red. Women flocked to see it and the day following a matinee neighborhood dressmakers would be driven almost to madness trying to follow crude pencil designs or verbal descriptions.

Not only Anna's stage clothes were copied. At least once a week Ziegfeld made page-one pictures or stories in the papers with some new furbelow of Anna's — or his. She had coats of sable and pearls that were famous. She wore jeweled garters and shoes the color of her gowns, usually of satin with silver heels studded in diamonds and rubies, and her house slippers always were set with sapphires. She wore corsets of rose point lace and each hook fastened under a ruby with rosebuds nestled in a *chou* of lace. Her evening gloves were laced with silken cords, and as she sped along in her automobile her tiny hands grasped the wheel in white kid, the scarlet cuffs hooked with gold clasps.

While her waist couldn't be small enough, her dresses couldn't billow enough for Anna. She wore petticoats sewn with flounces and flounces of

Will Rogers with Billie Burke, Ziegfeld and Patricia

INTERNATIONAL NEWS PHOTOS, INC.

INTERNATIONAL NEWS PHOTOS, INC.

Florenz Ziegfeld shortly before his death.

maline, and the chiffon and lace which were the petticoats themselves were caught with tiny bunches of flowers here and there. Her jewels were sensational; they were also to be her fortune and security: diamond necklaces, earrings, pendants, bracelets, brooches. Next to diamonds, pearls were her delight.

An appraisal of her estate after her death disclosed gross assets of $257,859, for the most part in jewels. A famous $100,000 necklace was sold for $52,000. There was another pearl one valued at $40,000; a lavaliere, $15,000; a diamond collar, $12,000. In this she showed herself smarter than the man who made her. Ziegfeld died virtually without a dime.

Milk baths and such stunts were fine enough in their way, but the daring idea that really projected Anna into her position of public adoration was an authentic bit of Ziegfeld inspiration. After her first appearance in this country in *Parlor Match,* followed by *Papa's Wife,* Ziegfeld got busy with plans for *The Little Duchess.* It was then that the flash of inspiration struck. He would surround Anna with tall, beautiful, stately girls, to bring out the gay abandon of her diminutive charm.

This was a tremendous challenge to confront her with, but Anna met it and triumphed. When "the nymphic Anna of the amber eyes," as one hypnotized critic put it, opened at the Casino, "she pitted her beauty against a dozen others." There were twelve lissome, svelte and gorgeous girls, he said, in a trance of ecstasy, all of them with the beauty of a Lillian Russell. In fact, they were so overpoweringly beautiful that the audience gasped. But little Anna more than held her own. "Most stars squirm at too radiantly lovely opposition, but not Anna," the critic said breathlessly. "The milk has not curdled nor condensed in her baths . . . Anna always revolutionizes everything she does."

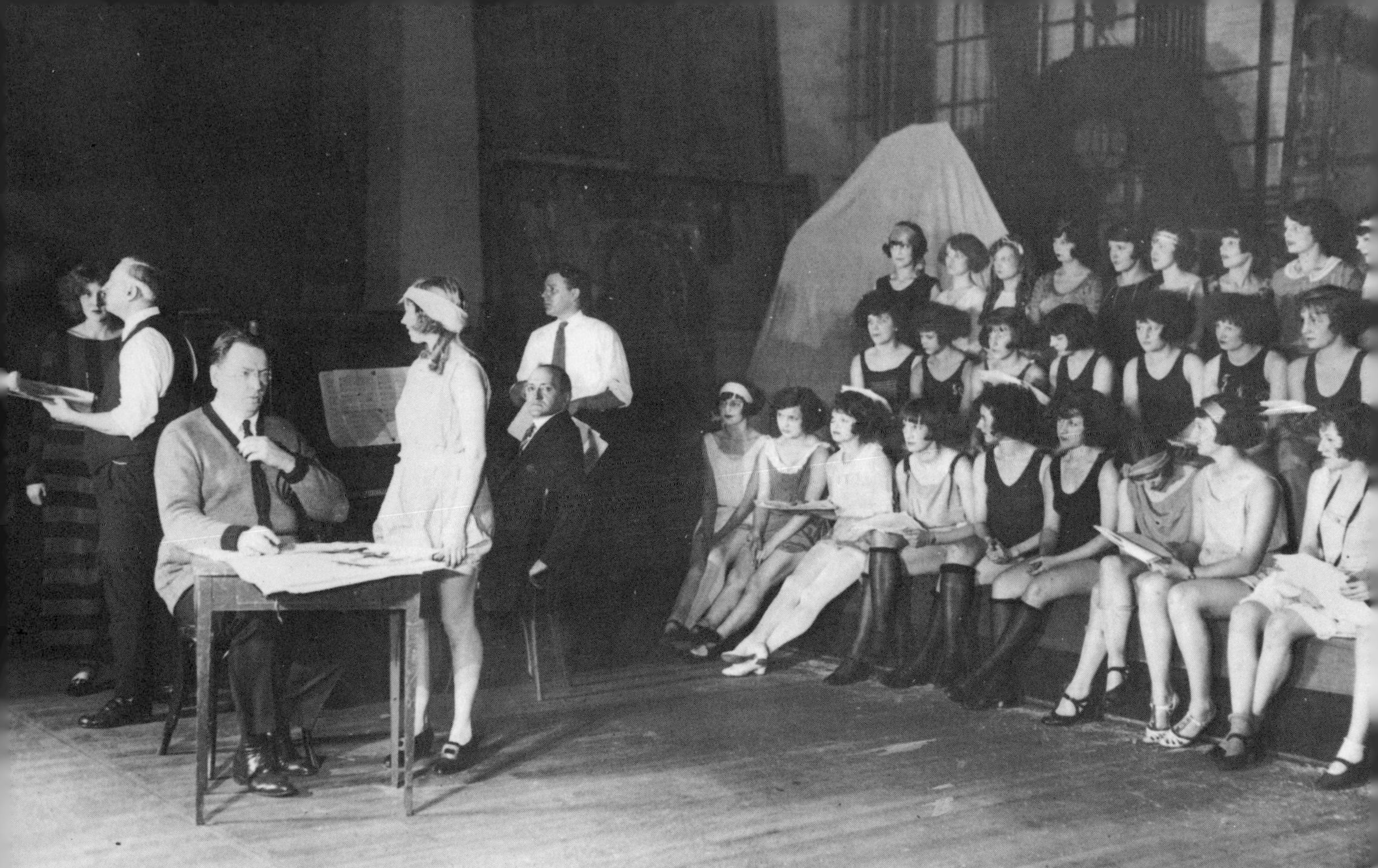

INTERNATIONAL NEWS PHOTOS, INC.

Ned Wayburn directing the girls in the 1923 Follies

What Ziegfeld really improvised was a kind of sensual concerto, with Anna the solo instrument of desire against a background of seduction. The show was a sellout all the way through, and on the occasion of the 100th performance Ziegfeld presented every lady in the audience with a silver-topped cut-glass powder jar. It was inscribed, naturally, with Anna's name.

He used the identical technique in *The Parisian Model* and *Mlle. Napoleon.* It was in the former production that Ziegfeld first presented the illusion of nudity on the legitimate stage without actually showing it. The sensational scene that lured men about town time and time again to the show depicted an artist's studio. Six girls in long cloaks stood before easels; that is, the easels were between them and the audience. Suddenly the girls threw off their cloaks and the audience saw gleaming bare shoulders and curving bare legs. The psychology was perfect, and the logic of the illusion proceeded like this: (a) this was an artist's studio; (b) artists paint beautiful young women in the nude; (c) hence when the girls threw off their cloaks they were nude. They weren't, of course. They wore strapless evening gowns with the skirts and trains pinned up. The audience didn't know this. The audience didn't want to know. It wanted to believe the girls were naked, and Ziegfeld graciously and profitably was only too glad to supply the impression.

All these exercises in ingenuity were inevitably leading up to his masterpieces, the Ziegfeld Follies. He was beginning to understand the pattern, partly compounded of the Folies Bergère formula from Paris plus his own almost invulnerable sense of showmanship.

Such was the success of *The Parisian Model* that it ran a year. During that time Ziegfeld looked over the musical comedy and revue field and found it lacking in costumes and girls. Generally the recipe was about twenty girls, three changes of costume, a pair of young lovers, a leading woman with a voice and reputation, a straight man, dancers, a dozen or so musicians in the pit and the inevitable boy-gets-girl plot. In his months of study – he saw everything produced that season – he decided to change all that. He would glut the gourmets of excitement with a feast of desire.

The plot was to be insignificant and sometimes would not even exist. If there were to be a plot it would be a stage-door waif, for Ziegfeld dreamed of producing such musical comedies that the audience would be over-

PICTURE COLLECTION, NEW YORK PUBLIC LIBRARY

Anna Held before she came to America.

whelmed with beauty and magnificence, and whether the boy got the girl became academic. He always did anyway. And what was the sense of a plot in a revue?

In place of twenty girls of varied ages, some of whom could sing a little, some dance a little, he would have one hundred and twenty girls whose figures would be as provocative as their faces; tall, stately girls, radiant with youth and draped in priceless costumes of furs, gems, laces, ribbons and flowers, who would need only to walk with patrician grace before the foot-

Anna Held in *Papa's Wife* — 1899

INTERNATIONAL NEWS PHOTOS, INC.

INTERNATIONAL NEWS PHOTOS, INC.

Anna Held about 1900.

Anna Held and her bicycle.

INTERNATIONAL NEWS PHOTOS, INC.

lights. He envisioned these beauties dressed to represent the seasons, months, nations of the world, celebrated courtesans of history, grains of the field, leaves of trees, animals of the jungle, flowers of the garden — thus he first envisioned them and through the years his vision became reality.

He would put a hundred musicians in the orchestra. He would retain the greatest artists to design as many as twenty changes of costume for every girl. Where one comedian would amuse an audience, six would convulse it. His music would be sparkling and gay or as beautiful as the stuff of dreams and would leave audiences humming or whistling softly as they left.

The influence Anna Held exercised on Ziegfeld in his development toward the Follies is as conjectural as her past. But it must have been considerable, for she was not only shrewd but intensely devoted to him, and he, in his odd way, was devoted to her, although there were long and heartbreaking lapses when he went away physically, and equally distressing periods when he disappeared emotionally, wrapping himself in an armor of silence. Still, that was his nature, and that he did love her — at least in the first years of their union — there can be little doubt.

A point in case is the sentimental marriage ceremony they went through shortly after Anna arrived in America. It was apart from their official marriage. It was probably spontaneous. Ziegfeld had invited Anna and a few of his more intimate friends to dinner. When Anna made her entrance swathed in sable — and Anna knew how to make an entrance — she removed her cloak. There she was, a vision that only Ziegfeld or Anna could have dreamt up. Her gown was white, embroidered in long-stemmed lilies and leaves of white, green and gold. Around her neck was a chain with a diamond and pearl pendant valued at $15,000, and worn on her right leg was a diamond garter. But even the diamonds couldn't outshine the stars in Anna's eyes that night.

It was a gay affair and the guests dined on the finest of foods, with vintage wines, as they listened to the soft strains of a Viennese stringed orchestra. It was gay until Ziegfeld, during a lull in the music and conversation, took Anna's tiny hand in his and, to the amazement of his guests and perhaps even Anna, softly began: "I, Florenz, take thee Anna, for my wife." And, the sauciness in her eyes replaced by solemnity, Anna repeated in what amounted to a whisper, "I, Anna, take thee Florenz. . . ."

There are some who say that the official ceremony took place in Paris in 1897, and others who claim to have known that they were married secretly in New York in 1901. No one can say for a certainty where or when it took place. But that Anna truly loved Ziegfeld no one has ever doubted. Her love for him was a doting devotion, and Anna of the naughty eyes and gay songs was capable of giving that devotion to but one man. Anna was twenty-two when she met Ziegfeld and was married to Maximo Carrero, a South American tobacco planter almost old enough to have been her father. They

Anna Held in *La Poupée*

INTERNATIONAL NEWS PHOTOS, INC.

had one daughter, Liane, about whom little was known as at the turn of the century, and for many years afterwards, actresses were not supposed to be mothers. Carrero, learning that Anna wanted Ziegfeld, let her go. He died soon afterwards with what was described in the popular parlance of the day as a broken heart.

Anna and Ziegfeld lived together until August, 1912, when Anna obtained a divorce in the New York Supreme Court. By that time the Ziegfeld Follies had for five years been developing into the American institution they were later to become. It might have been the glorification of his beauties or simply that Ziegfeld's restless mind was too busy with other ideas and ideals and didn't have time enough for Anna. Whatever it was, she stamped her tiny foot too often to amuse her husband. Six years later, Anna died.

She died calling for the only man she had ever loved. Ziegfeld arrived at her bedside a few hours after her death. Anna, true to the publicity with which Ziegfeld had surrounded her, died from dieting and from cinching in the little waist that, along with her rolling eyes which "I Just Can't Make Behave," was her trademark.

Ziegfeld by this time was becoming an opulent individualist, with the glamor of his girls and the glitter of his Follies making a new chapter in the history of the American theater that lasted through the end of the roaring twenties.

PICTURE COLLECTION, NEW YORK PUBLIC LIBRARY

Anna Held after her separation from Ziegfeld.

chapter two

On July 9, 1907, Ziegfeld presented his first Follies to New York. It was a sweltering night and the little, listless breeze that occasionally drifted across the roof of the New York Theatre was like a dank and wilted caress. Even with the air-conditioning apparatus of today no showman of the present times would think of opening such a show on Broadway in midsummer unless he were touched with suicidal madness. But Ziegfeld employed a different, ageless, and perhaps more effective kind of conditioning, that of beguiling the curiosity and whetting the appetites of his audience.

For weeks he had been announcing through the press that the Follies was "Another One of Those Things, in 13 Acts," a supreme exercise in dramatic modesty that asserted by built-up innuendo what it pretended to deny: namely, that this was a show that combined the orgiastic rites of Carthage with the winsome sensuality of the early Renaissance, and if you missed it you might as well be dead, in fact, you *were* dead socially. The white tie and decolleté set snapped voraciously at the bait. What mattered the humidity when this spectacle of unexampled splendor would send their senses reeling beyond reach of atmospheric annoyance? Less than nothing.

In a way, they were right. We would say today that they were psychologically overwhelmed. Even the critics, reaching moistly for adjectives in the exhaustion of the afterglow, conceded in effect that here was an absolutely new type of entertainment and, finally tossing their thesauri in the wastebasket, said the only sane way to sum it up was to say it was . . . the

PICTURE COLLECTION, NEW YORK PUBLIC LIBRARY

The first Follies – 1907

Follies. They said other things, too, of course, for it is the curse of their trade that critics cannot be wordless.

The show cost Ziegfeld $13,000 to stage, and he read such items as these with pure delight: "Ziegfeld besides having tremendous convictions has spent money like water. . . . No man can put on a show like the Follies and be a piker. . . ." He was never that. Years later he was spending $300,000 to open his fabulous Follies and he would never settle for anything almost-as-good or just-as-good. It had to be the best. If a salesman showed him silk priced at five dollars a yard and another sample at thirty dollars he unhesitatingly picked the latter. Furs, silks, jewels, flowers – whatever were the ingredients of one of his shows – had to be the finest he could find, even if it meant sending to Paris for the hip-length silk stockings his girls wore. And they were never barelegged. Ziegfeld knew that legs sheathed in silk were far more alluring than legs in theatrical make-up.

He had as unerring an instinct for that certain quality that would make a star as he did for glorifying his beauties. He put Nora Bayes in his first Follies on the basis of this instinct. Success had pretty much evaded Nora until she came under the master's management. Ziegfeld, his memory as long as that represented by the jade elephant he always carried in his pocket, remembered the eighteen-year-old Nora putting her heart into singing "Down Where the Wurzbürger Flows" on the stage of the old Hyde and Behman Theatre in Chicago. It was one of the earliest of Harry von Tilzer's best-sellers and Nora helped make it so. Ziegfeld gave her a contract for seventy-five dollars a week, and the girl who later was to know world-wide adulation was only too glad to get it. Her pay had been fifteen dollars a week in Chicago.

As great as her fame became, Nora lived and died believing her voice was "terrible." She called it husky and unmelodious, and indeed it was husky. Hers was the original throaty voice, but it throbbed with personality and she learned to sell songs when others merely sang them. Born of Jewish parents in Joliet, Illinois, her name was originally Leonara Goldberg and she adopted Nora Bayes along with Irish ballads and Irish comic songs. "Has Anybody Here Seen Kelly?" was one of her greatest hits in a long, long line of hits. And how she sang it! Arms akimbo, she walked up and down the stage, lapsing into excruciating comical pleading as the errant Kelly failed to appear.

Nora was an overnight sensation in the 1907 Follies and Ziegfeld continued with her the publicity build-up he had innovated with such success

The first Ziegfeld show girls — 1907

PICTURE COLLECTION, NEW YORK PUBLIC LIBRARY

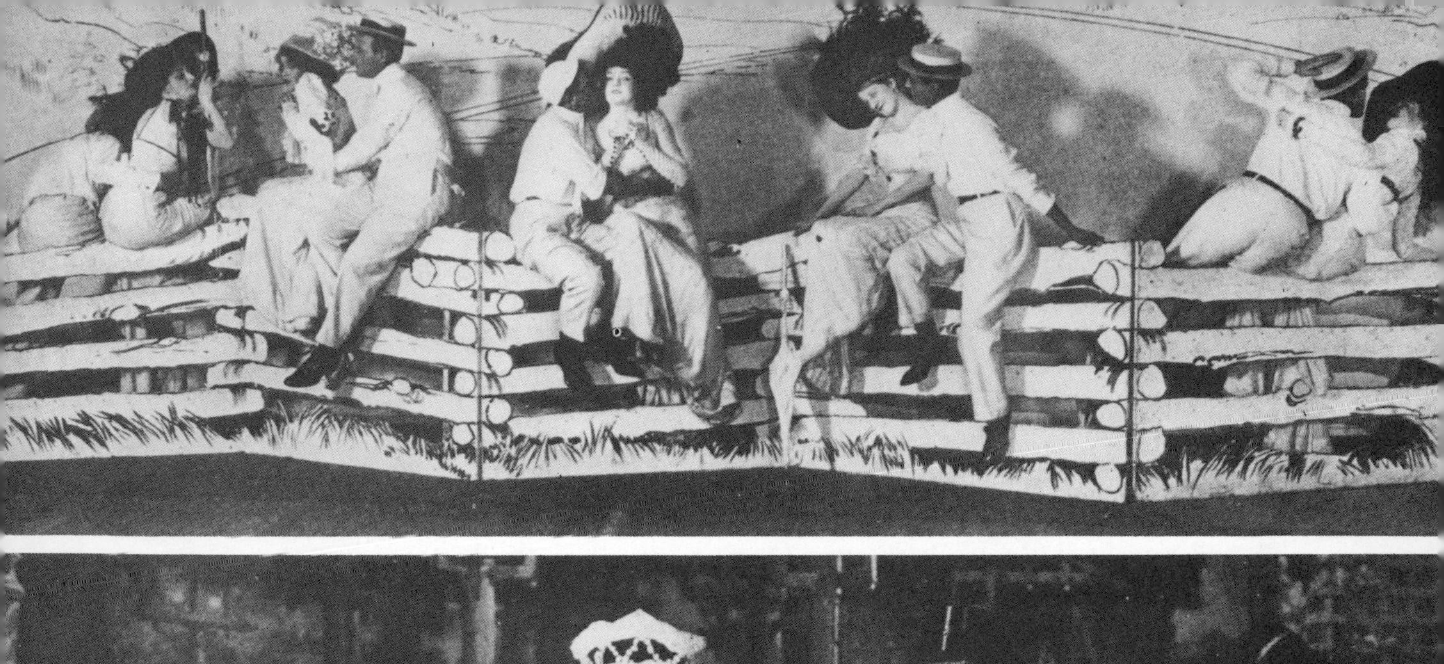

with Anna Held. This time it was lollipops instead of milk baths. Nora lapped one every three hours to keep up her strength, so the publicity said. The sale of lollipops didn't show an appreciable difference nor did the public evince much interest. Then Nora, or Ziegfeld, announced to a startled world that she ate one before each meal, to cut down on appetite and so maintain her figure. That did it. Women everywhere began buying lollipops, and the chocolates arranged artfully in their cut-glass bonbon dishes were emptied for the childish but chic candy that had until then been considered suitable only for the young.

By the time the 1908 edition of the Follies rolled around Nora was married to Jack Norworth, the second of her five husbands. Nora was a Ziegfeld star now and Norworth was one of Ziegfeld's most talented acquisitions, a temperamental one with whom he had considerable trouble. At one time after Norworth and Bayes had taken a walk out of Ziegfeld's custody he obtained a court order restraining them from appearing under any other management. But they were more than worth these eruptions of temperament. Norworth was not only an accomplished vaudeville trouper but he had a definite knack for lyrics. He wrote, for example, "Sing Me A 'Come All Ye' " and "You'll Have To Sing an Irish Song" for the 1908 Follies, and together he and Nora wrote the lyrics of "Shine On Harvest Moon," which became one of the great hits in the Bayes repertoire and later was to be repopularized by Ruth Etting after Nora's death in 1928.

There are innumerable stories of the beloved Bayes quips and they are perhaps best summed up by the philosophy by which she lived. "The greatest thing in the world is a laugh," she used to say, time and time again. This was not just a part of her Ziegfeldian build-up. Nora meant it. And she carried it, like a white banner, through success, her love for children which she could never have (she adopted three) and through the heartaches that must have accompanied the break-up of her marriages.

Nora was in and out of the Follies as she was in and out of vaudeville. It was when she was playing at the old Palace that she was dubbed "The Empress of the Two-a-Day." She'd leave vaudeville for Ziegfeld or a musical show but somehow she'd find the time to get back some time during the year to the two-a-day. One year in the twenties she took a flat in London to appear at a command performance at the Hurlingham Club for the then Prince of Wales. As she walked up the gangplank of the old *Leviathan* – London bound – the ship's band struck up the Wedding March for an obscure bride and groom. The young bride, clutching tight to her new husband's hand, blushed when Nora in her husky voice quipped: "That's my national anthem."

Nora loved the world and the world responded to that love. Laughing and gay, she never lost her enthusiasm for life or for singing. There are those who remember her and agree that she never quite achieved, in all her suc-

Scenes from the Follies of 1908.

PICTURE COLLECTION, NEW YORK PUBLIC LIBRARY

PICTURE COLLECTION, NEW YORK PUBLIC LIBRARY

Nora Bayes

cesses, the poignant winsomeness and the piquant charm of "Just Like A Gypsy." Others remember when George M. Cohan personally asked her to sing "Over There," the greatest of the flag master's first war songs. She did and it became the greatest seller in the country in the days of World War I. But there must be some also who recall with sadness and sentiment the last song she ever sang on a stage — or any place else. Nora was ill — how ill certainly she couldn't have realized herself, or perhaps she did and was making one last gallant gesture in a life that was filled with gallantry. Nora had promised Tom Noonan to go down to his Bowery Mission House and

INTERNATIONAL NEWS PHOTOS, INC.

Nora Bayes

INTERNATIONAL NEWS PHOTOS, INC.

Nora Bayes

sing for some of his derelicts. Her doctor insisted she go to the hospital that day for a tumor operation. Nora laughed at him and at Lou Alter, her pianist, who threatened to quit if she did what she dubbed "the Bayes Bowery stint." Nora sang four songs to an overwhelmingly enthusiastic audience, ending with "Alabamy Bound." She went from there to the operating table, but it was too late. Her destination was a lot farther than Alabama. Four days later the many thousands who loved her and cherished her gaiety learned that Nora, who thought trouble was put into life to accentuate happiness, was dead.

Nora's was the greatest name to emerge from that sensational 1907 opening spectacle. But she was merely the first of hundreds of greats that Ziegfeld built up over the twenty-three years of Follies and musicals with his superb blending of music, art, talent and beauty. Even his comics — and their names are legion — were surrounded by the magnificence of his sets or the beauty of his girls, who were the symbols of Helen of Troy, Venus de Milo, Aphrodite, Pompadour and all the mythical and legendary beauties of history. So that his audiences would not become satiated with elegance and grace, but rather would wait for these moments of magnificence, what better way to wait than with a good laugh?

Bill Shrode, Ziegfeld's stage manager for twenty-two years, says that one of Ziegfeld's favorite funny acts took place in the 1908 Follies. This was named "The Society Prize Fight" and in it were Harry Watson, Jr., George Bickell, Billy Reeves, Norworth and Shrode himself. It was a take-off on Philadelphia Jack O'Brien and Anthony Drexel Biddle. In those days O'Brien was teaching the socially prominent Philadelphian to box. Anytime they gave an exhibition in public, O'Brien quite naturally would allow Biddle to bounce him around a bit. Watson impersonated O'Brien and Reeves was Biddle. This act was responsible for the slang saying of the day: "Remember what I did to Philadelphia Jack O'Brien!"

That same year Bert Williams, one of the most beloved comics, made his debut under the Ziegfeld auspices. Bert, who was born Egbert Austin

INTERNATIONAL NEWS PHOTOS, INC.

Bert Williams

Williams, had only to come on-stage wrinkling his eyebrows and balancing on one foot when he reached the edge of the stage to send an audience into convulsions. In fact, it took only a wiggle of Bert's big toe to send them into a paroxysm of joy. His droll humor delighted thousands and they listened as he talked-sang "Nobody" and "Late Hours" and so many of the other songs that only he could, and did, put over.

One of the greatest comic acts of all times had audiences choking with laughter and nearly falling out of their seats in the Follies of 1911. It was called "Upper and Lower Level" and it was enacted by Williams and Leon Errol. The scene was the New York Central Depot, forerunner of today's Grand Central Terminal, and Williams played Rufus Redcap to Errol's Major Waterbrush. As may be surmised, Major Waterbrush had taken enough liquor aboard to float the Staten Island ferry. The act started with precisely four written lines and Williams and Errol carried on, as the mood led them, from there. The mood led them by the hilarious road of pantomime and ad-libbing farther and farther and longer and longer until finally they had stretched out the act to twenty-two minutes. This was when the Follies was playing in Chicago and Ed Rosenbaum, manager of the show, became alarmed and wired Ziegfeld that these two clowns were out of control and could not be curbed. "Curb them," telegraphed Ziegfeld in five or six hundred words. "Can't," came the reply from Rosenbaum. So Ziegfeld hopped a train and steamed out there with a symbolic hatchet in hand. He would cut that act down to size! But as he stood at the back of the theatre watching them he was laughing so hard the hatchet fell out of his nerveless hands. The act remained as it was.

While Williams was at the top of his career there occurred an ironic episode that perhaps is not without significance to sociologists, psychologists and other students of the human scene. The year was 1912 and Williams was making $1,400 a week at the time and convulsing the smart-set audiences. As a dare or a challenge, or maybe a bit of a lark, he agreed to appear at an amateur night at Miner's Bowery Theatre as an unknown amateur doing an impersonation of Bert Williams. He was introduced simply as Joe Martin. Williams strolled onto the stage with the familiar Williams' accessories of naïve and stumbling awkwardness verging on hidden panic. It very soon became apparent that the tough spectators at Miners considered that Williams was giving a dreadfully poor imitation of Williams. There were jeers from the floor and catcalls from the balcony and presently, as Williams kept trying, these changed to demands to "give him the hook." This was no metaphor at Miner's. There was a hook on amateur nights, standing just inside the wings. The demands became so strident and insistent that in order to prevent violence and riot Williams literally was given the hook. If there is a moral in this, it may be one of several: (a) never try to imitate yourself, (b) once you have achieved a name, never abandon it, (c) many a gag would fall flat but for the fame of the person delivering it. At any rate, it was an adventure Williams never forgot.

Ziegfeld and Errol remained in accord through many Follies and almost as many musicals except on one subject, girls. And what Errol had to say on this subject must have made the master squirm. Errol gave out countless interviews on the one general theme that beautiful girls were brainless. Further, he went on to say, beauty in a woman was not so much the gift of nature as the contrivance of man. He held that with proper lighting effects he could make any girl beautiful but that no showman's hocus-pocus could give her a brain. It may well be that Ziegfeld privately agreed with this thesis, but what disturbed the producer was that Errol was disclosing a secret of the trade and by so doing was depreciating the formula of the Ziegfeld technique. There is no way now of knowing whether Errol genuinely meant what he said — there is plenty of proof today that beautiful women and brains *do* mix — and Errol certainly was advancing a dubious generality that cast question on his own intelligence. Like most comedians from Moliére down through the years Errol was deadly serious off stage, but being deadly serious is not, per se, an indication of mentality. Whatever were the reasons, Ziegfeld preferred to ignore what he considered a strange quirk in the man who was to become one of his best known stars.

Leon Errol was born in Sydney, Australia, July 3, 1881 and started life with the idea of becoming a surgeon. He attended the Sydney University School of Medicine and Surgery, but a quarrel with a professor changed both his mind and his vocation. He played with a Shakespearean repertory company for two years until the lure of a passing circus attracted him. He became in turn an acrobat, a clown and an animal trainer; and soon after, a resident of San Francisco, California.

One of the parts Errol had played in Australia was that of Eccles in *Caste,* one of the most celebrated drunks in dramatic literature. He had had some success as a juvenile but basically his talent was in the musical field, and invariably he appeared as a red-nosed comic. His first job in San Francisco was in a beer garden where he sang coster songs that were followed by groans from the audience and a mass pelting with peanuts and popcorn. His eccentric dancing, however, was without an accent and caught the crowd's fancy. With his wobbly legs combined with his funny brows and funny eyes he was later to become the most hilarious inebriate ever to stagger across a stage. "Rubber Legs" became his nickname, and before he was through he'd played drunken sailors, husbands, cowboys, chefs and even a king in Ziegfeld's *Louie the 14th.*

Errol might have stayed on the coast except that the great San Francisco fire drove him to New York. By that time he had drifted into the burlesque field and was appearing in *The Lilies,* a frothy bit of entertainment he both wrote and directed and in which he was the principal comedian as well. A. L. Erlanger saw a performance and was so taken by Errol he decided he must have him immediately for a musical comedy he planned to produce called *The Primrose Path,* and accordingly paid $15,000 for his release. For some reason *Primrose Path* was never put on a stage, but while Erlanger was working on it, it was decided that Errol would work for Ziegfeld until he was needed. Errol made his Broadway debut in the Ziegfeld production of *The Winsome Widow* and while theatrical history wasn't made that opening night Ziegfeld, with his instinctive ability to recognize talent, refused to give him up. He put him next in the 1911 Follies, and off and on "Rubber Legs" appeared in most productions carrying the magic words — *produced by Florenz Ziegfeld, Jr.*

Artists and men about town found the stage of the New Amsterdam Theatre — where Ziegfeld had moved his Follies — a disconcerting Paradise as they clustered about the wings watching the beauties hurrying to the elevator which took them to their dressing rooms or dodging in and out of backdrops and sets. At least, those who were fortunate enough to get past the doorman did. For Ziegfeld frowned on this practice. The top-hatted, stage-door Johnnie, his arms laden with American Beauty roses, belonged, Ziegfeld said in no uncertain terms, outside, not inside, the stage door and woe to the girl who violated this rule. His beauties, statuesque, stately, and

PICTURE COLLECTION, NEW YORK PUBLIC LIBRARY

Lillian Lorraine — 1914

THE ZIEGFELD CLUB

Lillian Lorraine in the "Blue Devils" number – 1918

THE ZIEGFELD CLUB

Lillian Lorraine – 1918

aloof, did little but move across a stage with elegance and grace. That illusion, and it wasn't always illusion, was not to give way in the hustle and bustle of backstage life, nor were mascara-lashed eyes and near-nudity to be glimpsed from any point closer than the first row.

One of the few times in the history of the Follies when Ziegfeld allowed breath-taking loveliness to give way to buffoonery that almost approached slapstick was in the 1914 version. The action in one scene took place in a dancing school into which Leon Errol wandered with the mistaken idea that it was a Turkish Bath. As he staggered around the stage and tried with great bravado to focus his eyes on the dancing master, hopeful of getting a morning-after rubdown, the teacher ran out to call the cops. Enter twelve Ziegfeld lovelies for a tango lesson. "Do what I do," shouted the reeling Errol, his glazed eyes glancing with glee over the beauties. They staggered when he staggered, they rolled on the floor when he rolled on the floor and they sat down with a bang when he sat down with a bang. It was a clever satire (combined with a tangling of beautiful legs and bodies) and the audience shrieked with delight.

From buffoonery to beauty was only a curtain drop and Ziegfeld audiences' moods moved swiftly from glee to gasps with the changing scenery. The first Follies girl was born in 1907 and three years later she was recognized throughout New York, and a goodly portion of the country, as a dream of loveliness. Ziegfeld himself was giving interviews on "How I Pick My Beauties." Hardly a day went by without the press running a by-lined story of his as if they were chapters in a profound and monumental textbook.

Hair dyes? "Never. Nature is the best wigmaker and she knows what colors to mix." Color of eyes? "Anything but gray. Gray eyes can't be beautiful. They're too intellectual and belong only on a college girl." Figures? "Correct proportions count, of course, but I've had girls who weighed 145 pounds and looked like Venus." Women everywhere absorbed these bits on beauty and abided by them as they did Dr. Holt on the care and feeding of their children. As the articles were usually accompanied by pictures of some bared-shouldered beauty, the male members of their families showed more than passing interest. As time went on, Ziegfeld changed or at least modified his views on feminine loveliness.

But this was 1910 and the year that the first star Follies girl burst in a blaze of glory on Broadway. Her name was Lillian Lorraine and few other beauties had had so much written about them. Almost immediately upon her first appearance in the Follies, when she sang her famous "Swing Song," she became the darling of the Great White Way. Praise, money and jewels were showered upon her.

She dazzled what passed for café society at the time, although that name had yet to be invented, with a floor-length ermine evening wrap and the first ankle bracelet ever seen on Broadway. Her audacious bathing suits were the talk of the town and the scandal of Long Beach, Long Island. She was never without a gold vanity case initialed in diamonds, never during her heyday that is, for there came a time when she had to sell her jewels. Lillian lived in the grand manner and laughed at the world. She was the first of a seemingly endless bouquet of beauties picked by Ziegfeld from his garden of female loveliness, and she was the first of his girls to be dubbed by the master "the most beautiful woman in the world." Her charm, he said, was in her smile and her marvelously expressive eyes.

But Lillian's laughter at the world was the laughter of compulsive despair. She had a mania for speed and gay parties and a reckless insouciance that bordered on the psychotic, and it was not long before this girl, born in San Francisco under the name of Mary Ann Brennan, became known in the public prints as a "broken butterfly." She sold her jewels, estimated at $100,000, and was in bankruptcy and out again. She broke her spine in a fall on an icy sidewalk and recovered to undergo bouts with influenza and appendicitis. She was married twice to the same man and finally divorced for good from Frederick Gresheimer, son of a wealthy Chicago clothing store owner. Then she was married again, toward the end of her life, to Jack O'Brien, an accountant. Once she set fire to her boardinghouse room with a cigarette and was rushed unconscious to Bellevue Hospital. Another time the sheriff served her with a summons for running up a bill of $372 at Reisenweber's restaurant and walking out without paying it, although, of course, she had left the waiter a handsome tip. She was sued for alienation of affections. She was the Girl of Lost Chances and no outward regrets. She tried to make comebacks, and sometimes she succeeded after a fashion, but never did she attain the peak of acclaim that she enjoyed under Ziegfeld. Through all her troubles, many of them self-invited, she managed somehow to retain more than a vestige of the beauty that enchanted audiences in her Follies days.

When, after Ziegfeld's death, the Ziegfeld Theatre was reopened in 1933 as a Loew motion picture house, Lillian was one of the Ziegfeld-created celebrities introduced from the floor. Gus Edwards was at the piano on stage. Lillian was asked to sing her old song, "By the Light of the Silvery Moon." She walked to the stage and stood facing the audience, her hands clenched and her face working with emotion as Edwards played the opening bars. She opened her mouth to sing, but nothing came out . . . nothing but a sob as tears coursed down her face. She had to be led back to her seat in the audience. So while Lillian may have been the Girl of Lost Chances, she was also a warmhearted sentimentalist. In fact, that may have been one of the causes of her troubles. She lacked the shrewdness of Anna Held, and she left her heart in many places. Lillian died in 1955 at the age of sixty-three. In her time, she was a great and glorious beauty.

Lillian Lorraine — 1921

INTERNATIONAL NEWS PHOTOS, INC.

Lillian Lorraine

PICTURE COLLECTION, NEW YORK PUBLIC LIBRARY

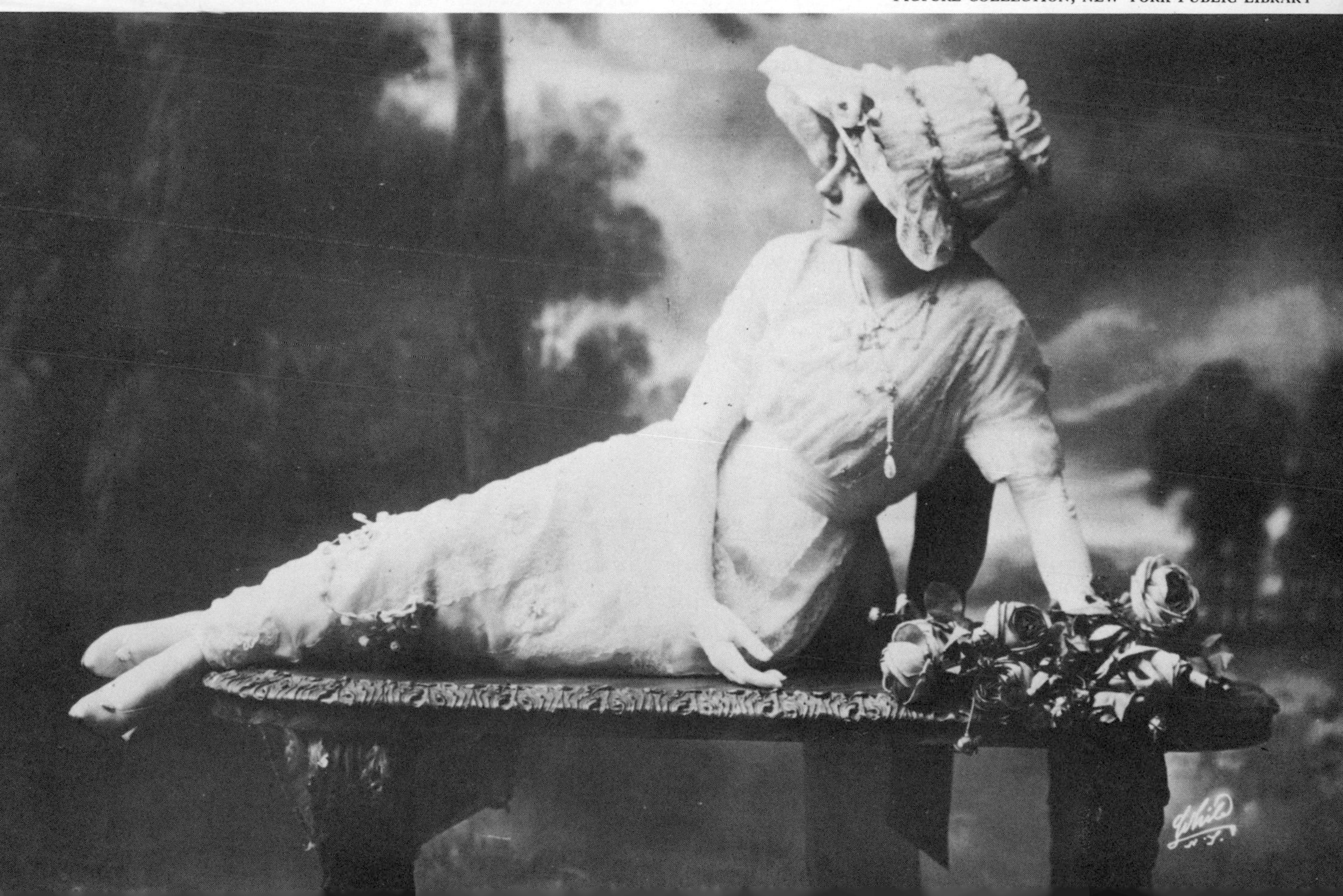

chapter three

Loveliness remained Ziegfeld's chief objective always and yet by some strange twist of fate a thin, widemouthed girl with scrawny legs and no figure to speak of became perhaps the greatest of his great stars. She was Fanny Brice, and her expressive eyes and quick mind made her one of the most famous mimics of all times. Fanny, in the tradition of famous comics since time immemorial, had the ability to bring an audience from tears of melancholia to tears of merriment. She could, in the opinion of millions, do anything. And this talent gave her an inward beauty that must have been the envy and despair of many a beauty who had little to offer but perfection of features and a perfectly proportioned body.

This undefinable quality of Fanny's must have been what Ziegfeld recognized when he heard her sing "Sadie Salome" in Seamon's Transatlantic Burlesque in 1910, and he immediately hired her for his Follies. Irving Berlin wrote "Sadie" and suggested to Fanny that she sing it with a Yiddish dialect. It was screamingly funny and yet filled with pathos; a gift Fanny was an expert at. From that time on her name was almost inseparable from the Follies and there was a prevailing conviction that a Follies wasn't authentic without Fanny.

Sometimes she was ribald, but her sense of caricature was always brilliant. She lampooned evangelists, cockneys, ballet dancers, fan dancers, duchesses and Indians. She moved about on her thin legs and there didn't seem to be an end to the absurd expressions she could bring into her face.

As one critic remarked: "With her undisciplined sense of the ridiculous and her mobility of features, she makes herself a handsome woman — more than she has a right to be."

Fanny traveled the traditional — or so it seemed of theatre people in that early era — hard road that led from New York's Lower East Side, through the various neighborhood variety theatres to the pinnacle of the times, the Ziegfeld Follies. She was only thirteen when she entered an amateur-night contest at Keeney's Theatre where she sang in a scared childish treble "When You Know You're Not Forgotten by the Girl You Can't Forget." She won the first prize of five dollars, which was augmented by three more thrown onto the stage by a wildly appreciative audience. So heady was her success that she quit school and changed her name from Fannie Borach to Fanny Brice for theatre marquee purposes, although Fanny was the only one who believed her name would ever get on one. "I never could spell," she remarked long after it was spelled out in bright lights.

She was born on the Lower East Side on October 29, 1891 to Charles Borach, an Alsatian saloonkeeper. Her mother, Rose, a Hungarian, brought up Fanny, another daughter and two sons, and made the free lunches that adorned every bar when a schooner of beer cost a nickel. Unlike many other stars, Fanny never tried to conceal her underprivileged background. The stories of young Fanny singing for pennies in back yards, dancing on the saloon bar, or cadging her way to Coney Island and home again remained

INTERNATIONAL NEWS PHOTOS, INC.

Fanny Brice — 1920

PICTURE COLLECTION, NEW YORK PUBLIC LIBRARY

Fanny Brice with a rising young comedian — Bob Hope — 1936.

always, embellished perhaps as the years went on, affectionately in her mind and pleasurably in her conversation.

There are some hackneyed and hurried historians of the theatre who would have you believe Fanny's first professional appearance was as a member of the chorus in the George M. Cohan–Sam Harris musical, *The Talk of New York*. In a quibbling sense they are right, but in a real sense they are wrong. It is true that after rounds and rounds of amateur nights where Fanny by then was picking up as much as fifty dollars a week from coins tossed at her feet, she was engaged for the chorus of the show. But Fanny never appeared the opening night, nor thereafter. In fact, she never got beyond the first day of rehearsal.

Ambitious and wanting to convince Cohan and Harris she could sing, she held the last note of "Won't You Put a Little Bet Down on Me" long, long after the rest of the chorus had finished. She clamped a kind of quavering lien on that last note. Perhaps she was waiting for the clink of coins she was used to, or it is remotely possible that she was too frozen with fear to be able to stop, but whatever it was she heard a snappish voice shouting: "You there! Go back to the kitchen." Fanny fled to the basement to the obbligato of the venomous snickers of the rest of the chorus. Two hours later she crawled out ashamed, with the searing shame of the very young when they have been ridiculed. She went home, her pride in shreds, but stitched it together sufficiently to announce to her mother: "I didn't get the job because I was too skinny." Twenty years later Fanny was hired, not by Cohan who had caused her anguish, but by Harris for his Music Box Revue at a salary of $2,600 a week.

Fanny went from that early debacle to a job singing in an 83rd Street stereopticon parlor which was short-lived because a chance to play an alligator in a touring company of *A Royal Slave* came along. Back in New York she talked her way into an eighteen-dollar-a-week job in Seamon's Transatlantic Burlesque. She couldn't dance so she was hired to sing – up in the gallery, backstage, any place where the audience could hear but not see her. She wasn't allowed on stage because she wasn't a regular member of the chorus. She couldn't be, as burlesque required in those days a buxomness of beauty and a slithering walk plus a smattering of dancing ability. Fanny had none of these attributes. But Fanny had ambition, a hard-driving burning type of ambition and a tremendous sense of the comical, so she bought herself a pair of wooden shoes to fit her awkward feet to rhythm. And finally she got a two-dollar raise and a chance to displace the company's soubrette, a fattish woman who was beginning to affect the gentlemen who stared at the runway about as much as a stale stein of beer.

After Ziegfeld came, saw and was conquered by Fanny's hoydenish hilarity in Seamon's Burlesque and seized her for his own, the rehearsal stage once more was nearly Fanny's undoing. Abe Erlanger of the producing team of Klaw and Erlanger, with whom Ziegfeld had joined forces to produce the first Follies, had assigned to himself the role of director of diction. Erlanger was not, I hasten to add, trying to impose on the members of the cast a Beacon Hill accent, but he wanted the words, particularly of the songs, to get across to the audience distinctly, as those of the better singers of jazz and popular songs do today. He was right, of course, since it is only in the Alpine forms of culture, such as opera and the concert stage, that audiences have been conditioned to expect a singer to be more or less unintelligible.

At any rate, Fanny was on stage singing and Erlanger, snuggled in an orchestra chair, did not think she was putting it over. He climbed to the stage and tapped Fanny on the shoulder. He was a small, rather plump man, with none of the popular physical appurtenances one associates with brass. Fanny tried to wither him with a look, and kept on singing. He tapped her again. This time she shrugged away his forefinger. When he tapped her a third time, Fanny thrust the palm of her hand full in Erlanger's face, much like a halfback avoiding a tackle, and shoved hard. It was not until she finished the song and was wandering toward the wings that she learned she had been mistreating the great Erlanger. It is to his credit that he did not fire her. The song that Fanny had been singing, by the way, was "Lovey Joe," which earned her twelve encores on the opening night of the Follies and really put her on the path to fame.

Fanny's first contract for the Follies stipulated a salary of seventy-five dollars a week, which was forty dollars more than she had been getting in burlesque. The contract was on stiff calendered paper, but Fanny was so enraptured with it that she fondled it into rags in a week. So Ziegfeld gave her another, same terms naturally, and Fanny wrecked that too by clutching it to her bosom and showing it to friends. In all, she had seven contracts before the show opened, which is about as apt an indication as I can give you of the overwhelming ambition of this gawky East Side girl, and her equally overwhelming love for the theatre. She never lost either.

But Fanny was more than just a singer, as Ziegfeld soon found out. Her classic burlesque and her artistry of satire became as much a part of the Follies as sensual allure. Her lampoon of sultry Theda Bara, the silent movie vamp, her take-off of Camille with W. C. Fields, and her wonderful comic version of the dying swan ballet were a part of the repertoire that made Fanny known as "a burlesque comic of the rarest vintage." She was billed with Eddie Cantor, Will Rogers, W. C. Fields and the other top Broadway names she appeared with through the years – appeared with and more than held her own. She toured throughout the country in the Follies, in the Music Box Revue of 1924, *Sweet and Low* and Billy Rose's *Crazy Quilt*. People laughed at her and Fanny loved it.

But Fanny's greatest success came from a song, a song that was sad and heartrending and appealed to every woman who had ever been in love and lost that love. It was in 1921 that Ziegfeld, again with his almost unbelievable and canny instinct for knowing what would have audience appeal, asked Fannie: "Do you think you can make them cry?" With that he handed her the song "My Man." It was a translation from the French song, *"Mon Homme"* to which Channing Pollock had written the English words. Fanny made them cry all right as she stood on a partially darkened stage in a plain black dress under what was supposed to be a French street light and sang wistfully and forlornly "Oh! My man, I love him so . . ." She popularized "Rose of Washington Square," "Second-Hand Rose," and on the lighter side "Becky Is Back In the Ballet," "I'm An Indian," and a score or so more; but she never again reached the heights of "My Man" and there was good reason for it.

The reason was that the song came straight from Fanny's despairing, fiercely loyal, love-torn heart. She was married three times but there was only one man she ever really loved, and he was a handsome, debonair heel named Nicky Arnstein. Her first marriage, for reasons that no one ever understood, including Fanny, was to Frank White, a barber in Springfield, Massachusetts, whom she met in 1911. It didn't take from the start; in fact, it lasted only a few days, and a year later it officially ended. In 1918 she was married to Jules W. (Nicky) Arnstein, born in Norway under the name of Wilford Arndt Stein. In a self-revelatory moment some sad years later Fanny told an interviewer, "He stood for manners, education, good breeding and an extraordinary gift of dreaming."

The trouble was Arnstein dreamed the wrong things. The year after their marriage he was arrested in connection with the disappearance of $5,000,000 in bonds stolen from a bank messenger. He was tried and convicted in Washington, D.C., and after a series of tactical defensive delays was taken to Leavenworth to serve a two-year sentence. Fanny would not believe that Nicky could have done anything wrong. She *could* not believe it. Her heart would not let her. When he was accused of masterminding the bond theft, Fanny remarked, "Why, he couldn't mastermind an electric bulb into a socket." She stayed by him during his imprisonment. She bore him two children. And she still loved him when she divorced him in 1927. By this time Arnstein, whose good manners and breeding were only on the surface and who had no conception of loyalty except as an abstraction beyond his interest, was using his "extraordinary gift of dreaming" toward another woman.

Two years later, in 1929, Fanny was married to Billy Rose, who then was engaged in producing Broadway revues and exposition spectacles. This was a pleasant enough union, although Rose sometimes showed signs of resenting being "Mr. Brice." At any rate, she divorced him in California in 1938, freeing Rose to marry Eleanor Holm. At the time Fanny said, "So now my third marriage ends and believe me, dearie, it's my last. I'm tired."

She was the anomaly of a one-man woman who married three times, and she really was tired. But she kept on working, as well as concentrating her leisure time on such things as hypnotism, art, and interior decoration. She had a large collection of children's paintings, she encouraged talented youngsters, and she decorated the homes of Eddie Cantor, Ira Gershwin, Katherine Hepburn and Dinah Shore. On the professional side, she had created the hilarious "Baby Snooks," a creation that endured through a great many years on stage and radio and once caused her to say, "It's like stealing. I don't have to work into it, it's part of me." And she was right. Baby Snooks was the child that always lived with Fanny, impulsive, wistful and sometimes maddening. When she died at fifty-nine in Hollywood in 1951, she had an eighteen-room house with, naturally, a swimming pool, a lot of money, a host of friends, and let us hope she had attained in the last years an inner peace; and that an armistice had been worked out between Baby Snooks and a mature and intelligent woman.

That was a memorable year, 1911, both for folly and the Follies. On the side of folly on the grand scale there was the theft of Leonardo da Vinci's "Mona Lisa" from the Louvre Gallery in Paris (it was recovered two years later in Florence) and on the side of the Follies, it marked not only the emergence of Fanny Brice, but of a girl who, in the conviction of many avid male observers, made Mona Lisa look slightly humdrum. She was Vera Maxwell, who burst upon the Broadway scene with what we would call today the force of an explosion measured in megatrons.

She was eighteen when she came under the Ziegfeld banner and nobody suspected in all her young loveliness that she was someday to introduce the world to the fox trot, that Victor Herbert and Irving Berlin were to collaborate on music for her, or that she would become involved in an international controversy about whether she was the most beautiful woman in the world. To the baldheaded rows who came night after night to see her, and the young men about town who came as often as their allowances or salaries would permit, she was the most beautiful woman in the world and who cared if she could dance or sing? They were there to look at Vera, in whom they found a combination of Guinevere, DuBarry and Récamier, and they never doubted for an instant that the originals who made heart-history were only half as lovely.

Vera was born in New York City, the daughter of William G. Maxwell, a well-to-do attorney who shrugged off his young daughter's pleas for dancing lessons and insisted that she was to go to Vassar and take her place in society. Vera taught herself to dance secretly by watching a step, or a graceful motion, and practicing it before the mirror in her bedroom behind closed doors. When she was fourteen the family fortune was wiped out, which meant to the young girl little more than a chance for a whack at her dreams.

INTERNATIONAL NEWS PHOTOS, INC.

Vera Maxwell

She ran away from home and got a job in the chorus of a traveling show. A few years later her father came into some money and wanted her to come home, but Vera, with a taste of show business and a remembrance of poverty and insecurity, stayed in the theatre. She danced and she laughed, but all the time the ghost of her poverty-haunted past, brief though it was, stalked her. She made a pledge with her best friend, Fanny Brice, in the Follies dressing room that if either of them was ever broke the other would come to the financial rescue. Fortunately neither of them ever had to.

Almost from the time Ziegfeld saw her and immediately put her in his Follies the cameo-featured beauty embarked on a life of success and riches. It is difficult to say which she valued more, but certainly she was as greedy for the security that money brings as a hungry child is greedy for food, and certainly her few years of poverty furnished a psychological motivation for placing money above fame. Perhaps this is part of the reason why she never married. The only man she ever loved was already married and a devout Roman Catholic. Vera could never have married him had he gained his freedom via the divorce courts. She wanted no one else. And husbands are likely to be financial risks. Beauty and allure were her assets and she took the greatest possible care to insure that they received the greatest possible returns. Loneliness she could endure, but poverty remained a ghostly terror.

She did little the year of her Ziegfeldian debut but walk on stage, proud, poised and shining in her aura of loveliness. But the week before the opening of the 1912 Follies she and Leon Errol introduced "The Seasick Dip," a dance that was described as a whirling maze. "Before the dancer is half through it he, or she, will find that its title is no misnomer." The dance, after three weeks of rehearsals by Errol and Vera, made its first formal appearance at an elaborate party given by Mrs. Charles Phillips Hatch in her Newport villa. It soon caught on with what was called the smart set before the first World War, and as one society editor put it: "This oddly named terpsichorean conceit is likely to have a much greater vogue than any other dance which has been in favor in the world's richest watering place."

As her fame grew so did her bank balance, and Ziegfeld helped make it so by letting her work at the Palace where she was paid as much as a thousand dollars a week. She went into *The Century Girl,* with music by Berlin and Herbert, and with her partner Wallace McCutcheon she introduced the fox trot. McCutcheon fell in love with her — as did almost every man who met her. The year was 1914 and Vera's name was coupled with a wealthy man of the times. Wallace, in the best romantic tradition, ran off and enlisted in the British Army. He rose to the rank of captain and for heroism in action won the Victoria Cross.

Then Paul Hélleu, a French artist whose etchings of women were the rage among the wealthy, came to America, announcing in a shipboard interview that never would he paint an actress — their beauty was too, too artificial. That was before he went to the Follies and saw Vera. Saw her and would not take no for an answer. He had to do her portrait. She was, he told anyone and everyone he talked with, "the most beautiful woman in the world." The press picked it up — Ziegfeld saw to that — and in London, Sir Philip Burne-Jones heard and scoffed publicly in the English and American newspapers. Gladys Cooper had just come to the attention of Londoners as a British dramatic actress. "She is the most beautiful woman I have ever seen, incomparably more beautiful than any American whose charms have been represented in this controversy," said Sir Philip with upper-lip inflexibility. The matter raged on but it was never settled; Miss Cooper went on to dramatic successes and Miss Maxwell grew lovelier and lovelier in each succeeding Follies.

It was at the height of her career that Vera met the man who, she repeatedly told Emma Ingeheuer, her maid, friend and companion, was the only man she ever loved. Vera never asked him to leave his wife but they saw each other regularly for a quarter of a century, until his death. In 1928, still lithe and lovely, she decided to quit while she was ahead. Her investments were sound — they rode out the stock-market crash — and her income was more than enough to live on comfortably. She was never bored. She learned to play golf and won many an amateur tournament; the only love left to her was the theatre and she saw everything that opened. Her charity work — particularly for those in the Follies who had not saved as wisely as

Vera Maxwell – The Blonde Venus

INTERNATIONAL NEWS PHOTOS, INC.

she — occupied most of her lonely hours. She died at only fifty-eight surrounded by the many paintings of her own beauty in her luxurious Park Avenue apartment. She died in the arms of Emma Ingeheuer, who was amply provided for in her will. Vera never had to fear poverty after her brief encounter with it. But she did have to fear the fear of poverty, which was her constant companion and must often have troubled her sleep in the long and lonely reaches of the night. But this is surmise. To paraphrase Anatole France's ironic condensation of the history of mankind: *she lived, she was beautiful, and she died.*

Compared to Vera Maxwell, Lillian Lorraine and the other lush lovelies of the early Follies, the Dolly Sisters, whom Ziegfeld found dancing in vaudeville and also hired for his 1911 edition, did not conform to the pink-and-white skin, full-bloomed figure that was the accepted prototype in beauty of that day. They were small and dark and exotic-looking, and their almond-shaped eyes and slim oriental grace made them a novelty. They were more like the glamor girls of today and Ziegfeld in his innate shrewdness realized they had something more than beauty, a tantalizing quality, a quality that was called "It" in the roaring twenties and today is known as "Oomph" or whatever you choose to call it. And it led them that first year under the master's magic touch to the enchanted interest of Diamond Jim Brady, to one millionaire after another, to wealthy marriages, and eventually to become almost the first of theatre names to be admitted into what was in those days the sacred circle of society.

Indeed, these Hungarian twins who grew up on New York's Lower East Side left a trail of broken hearts wherever they went, and they went from one side of the Atlantic to the other. They rose to fame by affecting identical costumes, hair-dos and perfectly matched steps though they were completely different in character. Jancsi, who Americanized her name to Jenny, was the romantic butterfly, reckless, gay and pleasure-seeking; Roszicka, or Rosie, was cautious, quiet, the more stable one. Jenny reigned over the gambling tables of Deauville and Monte Carlo, winning and losing sums that would have appalled even King Croesus. One New Year's Eve in Cannes she announced that her winnings amounted to 4,000,000 francs — and the franc was still worth five cents. Three of these millions she converted into the finest collection of earrings, bracelets, and enormous diamond and emerald rings that Cannes had ever seen. Then she went on to win 11,000,000 more, and it seemed as though her magic touch would never leave her.

Rosie shunned the limelight and spent large sums of her fortune in charity work and on rehabilitating orphans in her native Hungary, where her name became synonymous with Lady Bountiful. This is not to give the impression that Rosie didn't lead a gay, madcap, exhilarating existence. They both did, and it is only in comparing her life with Jenny's that one

You could hardly tell them apart.

INTERNATIONAL NEWS PHOTOS, INC.

PICTURE COLLECTION, NEW YORK PUBLIC LIBRARY

The Dolly Sisters – 1918

realizes Rosie was the more placid and peaceful one of the two. No one, not even Ziegfeld, could quiet what amounted to the passion of wanderlust that consumed the Dollys. He dressed them in white feathered skirts, diamond bodices and diamond headdresses, and always they whirled enormous plumed fans as their slim, graceful bodies moved in unison. But these gay dancing twins Ziegfeld skyrocketed to fame could never stay in one place very long. They left him eventually for a tour of England and the Continent, and finally became the stars of the Casino de Paris. In elaborately staged revues they introduced American jazz dances, the Charleston, the Black Bottom and the other novelties that were the passing rage in that Scott Fitzgerald era, and filled American expatriates living in France with more than a touch of nostalgia.

They bought a château in Fontainbleau and filled it with the titles of the Continent and the tycoons of America. They gave scrambled-egg parties which had the great and near-great yearning for invitations, just as Americans at home were yearning for the formally engraved card that would get them into an Astor or Vanderbilt soiree in New York. Through the Dollys' door, and into the sumptuous entrance which was lined with lighted jewel cases displaying their fabulous collection of gems, passed members of the smart international set. Europe's most eligible bachelor, David, the Prince of Wales (now the Duke of Windsor), became their semipermanent escort and trailed Rosie and Jenny to the spas of the Riviera or the Normandy Coast. Life was gay and meant to be lived with no thought of tomorrow. They were guests of Lord Beaverbrook and Sir Philip Sassoon, and the central figures at London's brilliant Liberty Ball where no less than eight couples masqueraded as the Dolly Sisters in plaid skirts and berets and Lord Ashley lost his bet that he could tell the real sisters apart.

They went off on country week ends with Sir Thomas Lipton and Sir Harry Lauder. Sir Thomas told them, "Married men make the worst husbands"; while Sir Harry added, "But actresses should marry from time to time." Then off to Deauville and the Casino to be visited by King Alfonso of Spain, gambling for high stakes and winning fantastic fortunes. In one season the twins won $850,000 from the Greek syndicate at Cannes as kings Christian of Denmark and Carol of Roumania watched and applauded. Jenny tripped off with the Vicomte de la Rochefoucauld to Sicily to visit the bandit, Romanetti; then back to Paris where the Moulin Rouge paid the sisters a record-breaking 3,000 francs a day — the great Mistinguett threatened to walk out unless she got 5,000 — and instead the Dollys quit and sued for breach of contract. They won, too, and were wooed back with the promise of a still higher salary.

Jenny amassed jewels in preference to husbands: a fifty-one-carat square-cut diamond ring, a priceless emerald necklace, a diamond necklace with a pear-shape stone dangling from the center — a collection that has been called the most valuable ever in private hands. Rosie married Mortimer B. Davis, Jr., son of the Canadian tobacco king who had married an actress himself but cut Rosie out by a clause in his will that cost her $65,000,000. A divorce reunited the twins again and sent them back to the Moulin Rouge and star billing with Maurice Chevalier.

Then tragedy struck, as it had a way of doing with terrific rapidity and terrible force to pleasure-loving, carefree little Jenny, who accepted luck as casually as she had always placed her chips on the green-felt gambling tables. Soon after the Dollys retired from the stage Jenny met and fell in love with Max Constant, a French flier. Theirs was a mad, wild love, full of many promises, heated quarrels and abrupt good-bys that never lasted. It was during one of these partings that she met H. Gordon Selfridge, the owner of London's famed department store as well as of many, many millions. At the time of their romance, and as such it was written about in the American and English press, a close friend of the Selfridge family announced that he

The Dolly Sisters in a later Ziegfeld show.

PICTURE COLLECTION, NEW YORK PUBLIC LIBRARY

had given Jenny $10,000,000 and a promise of marriage. Their projected merger brought Constant back into Jenny's life. Swayed between domestic security and the love she had for the flier, Jenny went with him for one last week end. Somehow it didn't jell, and as the lovers were motoring back to Paris in speechless silence their car was wrecked going seventy-five miles an hour near Bordeaux. Jenny nearly lost her life and suffered such severe cuts on her face and legs that she spent months in the American Hospital undergoing operation after operation for bone fractures, internal injuries and facial surgery. Rosie and the forgiving Selfridge rallied the world's most prominent surgeons to restore her beauty and they almost succeeded. But Jenny was broken in spirit. Rosie by this time had married Irving Netcher, a wealthy Chicago merchant, and they took Jenny home and married her to a Chicago attorney, Bernard W. Vinissky. But hard luck continued to follow the once-gay Jenny and acute melancholia drove her to hang herself in 1941 from a shower rod in her apartment.

Exactly one year later, to the precise day, Max Constant lost his life in a plane crash. Jenny left behind the twins she had adopted, Manzi and Klarika, children of a soldier who was killed in the first World War. Rosie lived on to see the story of the fascinating, fabulous Dolly Sisters made into a Hollywood movie. She led a satisfying life. As the more mature and stable of the two she was spared the dazzling heights of excitement that Jenny reached as well as the fathomless depths of depression into which Jenny sank. In Paris, when they speak of the sisters today, they talk mainly about Jenny and say: *"C'est la vie."* But they say it with sadness rather than with a shrug. For Jenny had the fascination of the fey. She was truly, as the description of that word puts it, under a doom and a spell.

A girl of another type in the early Follies, illustrating Ziegfeld's almost infinite variety of judgment, was sweet-faced Bessie McCoy, a dancer with whom Ziegfeld, along with all the theatregoers of 1908, had fallen in love when he saw her in her white-pomponned black velvet trouser suit (what we would describe today as coveralls) and her cone-shaped cap. This is not to give the impression that the master's infatuation for the pink-cheeked little dancer was anything but professional; but Ziegfeld's love whether it came from Ziegfeld, the man, or Ziegfeld, the producer, was all consuming and entirely possessive. Usually he got what he wanted — and he wanted merry little Bessie McCoy enough to more than double her salary. It came as no surprise to Broadway when the little star signed her name on a contract that already bore the ink-smudged signature of Florenz Ziegfeld. Although at that time the "Yama Yama Girl," as Bessie was known, would have been as welcome in any producer's office as Ethel Barrymore, who later was to become one of her closest friends.

Thousands came to see Bessie sing and dance as the Yama Yama Girl —

INTERNATIONAL NEWS PHOTOS, INC.

Bessie McCoy Davis — the Yama Yama girl

and then came to see her again. Almost from the night the opening curtain fell in the old Herald Square Theatre on the musical, *Three Twins,* the little dancer, born in the Mid-West of Irish parentage, became an overnight sensation. She was eighteen then and her tiny pouting mouth, her heap of yellow hair and her knack of dancing her songs became so effective that she often did them in pantomime with the audience filling in the words. Bessie could sing a little and dance a lot and who cared if she skidded off key, as long as her lithe body could enchant and delight as she moved across the footlights in what amounted almost to eccentric dancing? Bessie had reached success of sorts the year before Ziegfeld saw her and claimed her for his own.

Her nimble feet and her this-is-what-I-love-doing-most air had delighted Broadway the year before in *The Echo,* a musical comedy with a Deems Taylor score. When *The Echo* stopped reverberating, Joseph Gaites cast her for the part of the Yama Yama Girl, a role that became, and still is, synonymous with the name of Bessie McCoy. She had the world — as well as Ziegfeld — at her feet, literally. But she also had Richard Harding Davis, author, newspaperman and adventurer, bewitched as he sat in his first-row-center seat night after night and watched Bessie's twinkling toes. Bessie didn't know as she looked across the bright stage lights that the man who

Bessie McCoy Davis — early portrait

INTERNATIONAL NEWS PHOTOS

INTERNATIONAL NEWS PHOTOS, INC.

Bessie McCoy Davis

watched with such concentration was later to become her husband. She couldn't have known, for Davis was married at the time to Cecil Clark, a Chicago socialite and daughter of John M. Clark, president of a telephone company, and they had never met.

Their meeting in 1909 when Bessie was illuminating the Follies with the McCoy enchantment was a story that she told over and over again, as do most women who have loved and been loved. "I don't know whether it was luck or predestination that brought Richard and me together," she often pondered. "If you happen to believe that fate prearranges our lives then that was why I was in a music store on Union Square when Richard came in with a mutual friend. On the other hand, if it was luck alone there's nothing to prove that I wouldn't have met him if I hadn't gone into that shop. I don't believe it was chance — it was too big and too glorious a thing." Bessie from that moment on was in love, in love with a man she didn't and couldn't marry until 1912 when his divorce was a mild *cause célèbre* in the press.

Davis meantime was spending his nights watching Bessie on stage or sitting in her dressing room between numbers. By the time the 1911 Follies was drawing to a close — Bessie was singing "Take Care, Little Girl," dancing the main Daffy in Tad's Daffydils (a sketch taken from the famed Hearst cartoonist Thomas A. Dorgan's drawings) — Davis and Bessie were planning their wedding. They were married in the law office of William C. Rungee, a justice of the peace in Greenwich, Connecticut, with Ethel Barrymore and Gouverneur Morris as their attendants. A daughter, Hope, was born to them three years later and Bessie lived in quiet domesticity, running her home in Mt. Kisco, New York. When her husband died suddenly four years after their wedding she returned to the stage — and Ziegfeld — as Bessie McCoy Davis, in *Miss 1917* at the Century Theatre, described as a girl-and-music show.

The critics were kind to Bessie as she hung high above the stage suspended in a mechanical device representing Joseph Urban's conception of the moon. Before Bessie was swung out over the stage in her Urbanized moon the entire cast wished her well with embraces that were sincere to the point of badly crushing her costume. And when she was lowered to the stage and stepped from her brightly lighted moon to begin whirling about the stage with her old fantastic, acrobatic grace the applause was overwhelming. Bessie's blue eyes spilled over with tears. But her heart, while grateful, was still thoroughly domesticated. She missed Richard, and life with her small daughter was all she had to tie her emotionally to the husband she couldn't and wouldn't forget. She died when Hope was seventeen, in a hospital in Bayonne, France, where she had been taken from her villa at Saint-Jean-de-Luz several hours earlier. She left to her daughter $136,000 and the famous Yama Yama costume with the wish that: "Hope will wear it to a masquerade someday."

chapter four

Both to historians of world events and within the parochial confines of Broadway, 1914 was a big year. Archduke Francis Ferdinand was assassinated in Sarajevo, touching the match to World War I; the first ship sailed through the Panama Canal; and Woodrow Wilson was residing in the White House. In the Broadway sector no less exciting events were taking place. Ziegfeld had Ann Pennington, of the dimpled knees and long, dark hair, in the Follies; he titillated his audiences with his first apparent nude — Kay Laurell as "September Morn"; and he married Billie Burke, the red-haired toast of the town, thus embarking on a turbulent union that was to last eighteen years. Strangely enough she never appeared in a Follies production.

Miss Burke did not surrender easily. She had been brought from London to New York by Charles Frohman, a pudgy little man who was the King of Broadway and ruled his casts with an imperious hand, and she made her first appearance opposite the great, the impeccable John Drew, in *My Wife*. Frohman frowned at letting his young star dine with celebrities; he refused to permit her to use make-up off stage. If he could, he would have had her living in a nunnery. Frohman believed in protecting his property. But it was impossible to shut off Billie and her ravishments from the greedy world. Enrico Caruso met her, fell madly in love and proposed. Billie sweetly and firmly said "No."

Then Ziegfeld met her one night by way of an introduction by Somerset Maugham, when she had finished her starring role in *The Mind-the-Paint*

Girl. Probably for the first time in his life he knew the agonizing rapture of a pierced heart. He said, "Will you marry me?" and Billy said sweetly, "No." She said these sweet "Nos," she wrote these sweet "Nos," for a whole year while Ziegfeld bombarded her with flowers, telegrams and notes, and sent cases of pink champagne to her mother as a diversionary tactic to enlist her support.

Finally the sustained attack triumphed, the titian citadel of resistance was overwhelmed, and one afternoon, between the matinee and evening performances (it was a Saturday), Ziegfeld and his hard-won prize traveled quietly to Hoboken, New Jersey, by ferry and were married in the back room of a parsonage. The room was crammed with cribs and carriages, stepladders and buckets of paint. It was a setting that made mock of Ziegfeldian elegance. They returned to New York by ferry, standing hand in hand at the rail, and it is a fair surmise that it was the most wonderful water-crossing Ziegfeld ever experienced before or after.

They had a wedding supper at the old Hotel Brevoort and then Billie returned to the theatre and Ziegfeld to the New Amsterdam, a dazed and bewitched bridegroom who saw his wife's fair face superimposed on every one of his girls and who, for once, was not an alert sentry looking for a headdress that wasn't on the way he wanted it, or a run in a silk-sheathed leg. He was waiting trancelike for the time when he could take his wife in his arms and tell her what his heart wanted to say.

They managed to keep the marriage a secret for almost twenty-four hours, and when it did break in the papers on April 13th it shared page one with news of the execution at Sing Sing of Lefty Louis, Gyp the Blood, Dago Frank and Whitey Lewis for the murder of the gambler, Rosenthal. It was an ironic conjunction of passionate love and violent death, and Ziegfeld did not approve, for he had no appreciation of irony. Neither did Frohman who, seeking to break up the romance weeks before, had warned Billie that Ziegfeld was still in love with Lillian Lorraine, was still chummy with Anna Held, and in short, was not bridegroom material. So Frohman frothed and fumed . . . and was helpless.

There were, of course, the usual predictions, born of envy, anger and hope, that this would be a short-run marriage. There were some who said with what often passes for wit on Broadway that it would be scarcely more than a one-night stand. They were wrong for three reasons: this was genuine affection; Miss Burke and Ziegfeld shared in common the professional tradition of the theatre, so they had a deep and mutual interest; and Billie, behind her appearance of big-eyed naïveté, was a determined and intelligent young woman.

In fact, the tradition of the theatre extended for her farther back than it did for her husband. Miss Burke's father was Billy Burke, a famous clown. She grew up trouping, and while she was born in Washington, D.C., she spent most of her girlhood abroad, chiefly in London. It was her mother who christened her Mary William Ethelbert Appleton Burke and who never was on the stage. Mrs. Burke was the determining factor in making Billie a star, perhaps by way of compensating for her own lack of experience and talent. "My career," Miss Burke said once, "was the result of my mother's inhibitions. She wanted to be an actress and she never was, and she upset her family terribly when she married a circus clown." It was Mrs. Burke's ambition that led Burke to branch out from clown to vaudeville manager in England.

Among Billie's earliest memories were those of her singing teacher, Madame de Frotis, who assured Mrs. Burke (Billie was listening at the keyhole of the closed door) that Billie "had a voice" and should be sent to Italy to study. She never was, partly because family finances would not permit it and partly because Mrs. Burke was convinced that since her child had a natural talent it could be developed just as capably in England as in Milan. Another of Billie's memories was being instructed in acting by Charles Hawtrey, who had not then attained knighthood.

At that age, when all the world was green, Billie didn't care one way or the other whether she was to become a star. She loved life and she was gay, and she seemed to have almost a mystical feeling of security within her and a confidence that life would return her affection. It did. She was cheerfully willing to go along with her mother's ambition. She had no intense, desperate desire, and perhaps for that reason success leaped at her. She made her debut at the age of fifteen in an English music hall, doing an imitation of Edna May, a tremendous favorite of Edward VII, singing the Salvation Army Song, "Follow Me," from the musical *Belle of New York*. One year later she became a professional and by felicitous coincidence it was a role in *School Girls,* starring the actress Billie most admired, Edna May. Then the canny Frohman seized her for his own and brought her to New York. In an interview some time later Billie was quoted as saying that in the weeks before sailing she was so excited she could scarcely eat or sleep. I rather doubt that. It is not in character. I prefer to believe that Billie was pleased but not overcome.

Despite the storm raised by her marriage to Ziegfeld, Billie reported that they were "blissful despite the fact that our finances left much to be desired," since the grandeur of the Follies was costing her husband almost as much as they earned. Their finances might have left much to be desired, but that did not bother Ziegfeld one whit. Such trifles never did. In the red or in the black he insisted on living in the grand manner. But there were some trifles about her husband that bothered Miss Burke. She discovered to her horror that Ziegfeld wore long, peach-colored silk underwear. She heaved the whole batch away. Nor did she admire his other tastes in clothes — his too extreme Broadway-style suits, his inability to distinguish between good taste in dress and importunate exhibitionism — and she took pains to correct these faults.

Their marriage swung between scenes of red-haired fury and passionate peace. When she was angry, Billie screamed, threw china, tore draperies from the windows and attacked her husband with the nearest available weapon. Sometimes these tantrums were over her suspicions of Ziegfeld's interest in other women; after all, his business was beautiful women and it was not a business calculated to induce peace of mind in a wife. Billie didn't give a hoot for Ziegfeld's past interest in Lillian Lorraine or his past marriage to Anna Held, nor was she really fearful of any of the lovely women in his professional life — except one. That one was Marilyn Miller. Marilyn represented a real, formidable challenge, for Billy was convinced that Ziegfeld not only was enchanted by her but "idolized" her. So the two women were joined in a female battle to the death — to the death, that is, of one or the other's claim to Ziegfeld. Once in Boston Marilyn gave an interview saying Ziegfeld was frantically in love with her and would marry her if Billie would step aside. This was after the baby Patricia had been born to Billie and Ziegfeld, and Marilyn went on to say that Billie "waves her baby at him like George M. Cohan waves the American flag." Professionally, Billie recognized it as a smart line and said so, adding acidly that she doubted very much if Marilyn could have thought it up by herself.

Billie won that battle. She knew, she said, that Ziegfeld really loved her and she sent for him. It was not a rapturous reconciliation, but a tempestuous one. It was at this moment that Ziegfeld reached in a pocket and handed Billie a $20,000 diamond bracelet, which she hurled into a corner (and, of course, later retrieved). She won him from Marilyn but, as she said, lost him to a roulette wheel. She might have said innumerable wheels. They were a temptation he could not resist and they spun away untold thousands of dollars from him over the years. Yet Billie never let these faults break up their marriage.

It may be said that they loved one another in a curiously unconventional way. Yes, but their married life was never dull and it held together. And it is indicative that of all the compliments Ziegfeld paid Billie, the one she remembers most vividly is his saying, "Any girl who can wear a chinchilla wrap the way Billie can, and drag sables on the floor — she's for me." He was enchanted by insouciance and gaiety, and Billie gave him both, as well as diverting moments of rage.

After the 1914 season was over, Billie and Ziegfeld took a trip to California. In a way it was a kind of delayed honeymoon, but it was also the debut of Miss Burke in the movies and it was to stand her in good stead in the future. Thomas Ince offered her the leading role in *Peggy,* playing opposite William Desmond. Billie, incidentally, called Desmond "with his dark hair and deep dimples" the handsomest man she had ever seen. When the picture was completed Ince asked her to stay on for others, and Billie had to make a choice between a movie career and marriage. She chose the latter. (Of course, the legitimate stage had open arms for her, so it was not a clear-cut sacrifice.) Ziegfeld was starting something new, the Midnight Frolics on the Amsterdam Roof, and she journeyed back to New York with him and once more ran into the ire of Frohman. How could she cheapen herself, he asked furiously, by lending herself to so common a medium as the movies? Besides, they weren't here to stay anyway. Billie did not take this meekly. She answered him with cold and cutting scorn, and that was the end of relations between her and Frohman.

But if Billie would not stay West, Ince would come East. He opened a studio above a midtown livery stable and Billie agreed to star in a serial, *Gloria's Romance,* that was at the same time to be a super-epic and a colossal heartthrob. She never did, because while plans were in the formative stage she became pregnant and Patricia came along. It was directly after Patricia's birth that Ziegfeld decided that New York was all right enough in its way, but not the place for his wife and tender little blossom of a daughter. So he turned his attention to Burkely Crest, a retreat of vast acreage at Hastings on Hudson, upon which he spent $250,000 on a twenty-two-room, gray stone house, a separate ten-room house for Billie's mother to rattle around in, and a swimming pool designed by Joseph Urban. An enterprise like this naturally had to have some animal life, so presently it contained an elephant (a gift to Patricia), a herd of ten deer, two lion cubs and two bear cubs — all four of which became too dangerous for amusement after a while, a couple of buffaloes (briefly), cockatoos, parrots, partridges, pheasants, and a pony that had been ridden by the Prince of Wales.

This was the beginning of a period of affluence. There were even reports that Ziegfeld insisted that Billie rinse her beautiful red hair in champagne, but I am inclined to take these with a chaser of cold water. At any rate, Billie returned to making movies in New York, this time for the Famous Players-Lasky Corporation headed by Adolph Zukor, and also returned to the stage in *A Marriage of Convenience,* a hit. Ziegfeld was also doing fine. In addition to the Follies he was preparing and producing what were known as musical extravaganzas, among the first being *Kid Boots,* in which Eddie Cantor appeared. The equally great Will Rogers had also come under Ziegfeld auspices about this time.

These were good years, but they were to be followed by the bad. Good or bad, Miss Burke managed, miraculously some women thought, to retain her loveliness and the sheen of youth. It was not a miracle. It was the result of deliberate, careful planning, as one would plan to preserve an invaluable asset. Miss Burke did not throw her youth and beauty away; she put herself always on a rigorous regime of diet and exercise to keep both. When she was first married to Ziegfeld she used to do somersaults and exercises each morning. As she grew older she gave up the more vigorous exercise, but she still held herself to it in more moderate form and was always extremely conscious of diet. As a matter of fact, she spent a good portion of each day in the preservation of her loveliness, counting in the hours spent in salons for facials and massages and other such attributes of allure.

This practice, plus her movie experience, came to her rescue after Ziegfeld died in 1932 and left an astronomical pile of $500,000 in debts. She returned to the movies, this time in the role of the twittering, scatterbrained dowager (she made something like fifty pictures of this type), she appeared on radio, and she came back to Broadway in such hit plays as *The Marquise, Her Master's Voice,* and *The Truth Game*. She was and is a gallant person; gallant and loyal as a wife, gallant in her own relations with the world, and she has never lost that girlish love of life.

I have coupled Eddie Cantor and Will Rogers in this chapter because they were men of stature and mutual affection, and they rose to become not only great stars but distinguished citizens in the best of American tradition. It is not often in show business that a person rises out of the ranks of a star of the first magnitude to the more complex and infinitely more arduous duties of outstanding citizenship, but Cantor and Rogers did it. Their places of origin were very different, but their sense of responsibility was identical.

Cantor was born Izzy Iskowitch in the teeming Lower East Side of New York. Both parents died when he was a baby and he was brought up by his grandmother, Esther. If anyone was born a natural comedian, he was, but his wit was kind and his humor without sting. For it earned the neighborhood appellation of a "no goodnik." But on Hester Street this child was filled with joy of life, and no clothes however ragged and no shoes however scuffed could take this from him. He learned to do impersonations of popular stage personalities of the day and for this he acquired whatever pennies passers-by might deem to throw at his feet.

It is almost as if life, from the very beginning, had resolved to set him on the path to the self-fulfillment toward which most of the rest of us grope. But this denies the irrepressible tendencies that were within Cantor himself. He was not only destiny's child, he made his own, and he started making it when at sixteen he won five dollars at an amateur night at Miner's Bowery theatre. (How many others have had their start there?) He made his first professional appearance in 1907 at the old Clinton Musical Hall, which did not receive either the approval or the recognition of his grandmother. Next we find Cantor as a singing waiter in a Coney Island saloon, where his accompanist was the equally irrepressible Jimmy Durante.

Gus Edwards heard him in 1912 and gave him a job in his troupe called "Kid Kabaret" along with George Jessel, Eddie Buzzell, Georgie Price, Walter Winchell, Lila Lee and Gregory Kelly. Of such beginnings are stars

Will Rogers

INTERNATIONAL NEWS PHOTOS, INC.

INTERNATIONAL NEWS PHOTOS, INC.

Eddie Cantor in the Follies of 1917

INTERNATIONAL NEWS PHOTOS, INC.

Will Rogers in the first Follies in which he starred.

born. It was while touring with this vaudeville act that he met Rogers. They became friends, and later teamed again in philanthropic work. Something of surpassing goodness happened to Cantor in these early years. In 1914 he married his childhood sweetheart, Ida Tobias. They had five daughters who, with their mother, became nearly as famous as Cantor himself through his absolute adoration for them and the equally absolute determination not to hide that love within his heart. There is no question that this was one of the great, inspiring stage marriages of our time. They had their squabbles, of course, but Mrs. Cantor soon developed methods for keeping vehemence and recrimination out of them. She would hand Cantor one of their children

A typical Follies Beauty seems to be using her wiles on Will Rogers.

INTERNATIONAL NEWS PHOTOS, INC.

INTERNATIONAL NEWS PHOTOS, INC.

Eddie Cantor and Mary Eaton — two Ziegfeld graduates.

and say, "Here, Eddie, hold the little girl for a while." No man, especially one with the genuine sentimentality of Cantor, could hold out against this tactic.

Cantor's fame was rising. He was a success in London in a musical comedy, *Not Likely,* and returning to this country he teamed with Lila Lee in a vaudeville act. His first big break came in 1916 when Ziegfeld saw him in the musical, *Canary Cottage,* and seized him for the Follies. Cantor was in the Follies in 1916, '17 and '18, and it was there that three of the greatest comedians of that era, or any other for that matter, found themselves working together — Cantor, Rogers, and W. C. Fields. There is a semi-apocryphal legend that it was Cantor who tricked Rogers into talking while he was demonstrating his fabulous rope stunts. It is apocryphal in that Rogers had started to chat with his audiences a considerable time before, during his latter days in vaudeville. It is true that Cantor probably was the first to induce in Rogers the recognition that his personality and wit were of equal attraction to his rope — and were, of course, to become immeasurably greater. At any rate, the story is that before a performance one evening Cantor said, "Let's do something new, Bill. I'll give you a couple of lines in French, and just say them and see what happens." The lines, which were not precisely polite parlor French, brought a howl of laughter, and Rogers, in trying to explain in his Oklahoma drawl that he was not really an expert on the connotations of Parisian slang, was engulfed by successive waves of hilarity. So Cantor, at the very least, provoked the birth of a major wit.

Thereafter Cantor was to say of Rogers: "He's the most unselfish man I ever met. He never did a bad thing intentionally. If Will were alive today [this was in 1943], a lot of the confusion in Washington would have been kidded out of existence. He was the policeman of America — in his inimitable way, of course. I believe he was a great American."

Cantor was by way of becoming great himself. Cantor was on the threshold of stardom in the Follies, in fact he already had crossed it and was making thousands of dollars a week. But he was aware that many, many others were struggling along on much less and that their working conditions needed improving. And so Actors Equity was organized and a strike closed most of the theatres on Broadway. Cantor might have evaded this issue; there was no compulsion on his part to do otherwise except the sense of humanity to his fellow men and women that he has carried with him all through life. He became one of the leaders of the striking actors and this led him in future years to be a foremost partisan for Actors Equity, the National Vaudeville Association, and the Screen Actors Guild.

He also invited the hostility of Ziegfeld, who withdrew offers to star him. The Shuberts promptly signed Cantor for the lead in *The Midnight Rounders* which played for more than two years, and then in *Make It Snappy,* also a Shubert production. But Ziegfeld was not one to cling obstinately to hostility. He lured Cantor back with the lead in *Kid Boots,* one of the great Cantor hits. It ran from January, 1924, to December, 1926. His greatest stage success was *Whoopee,* which played from November, 1928, until March, 1930.

I don't think there is anyone who would argue that Cantor would make the Metropolitan Opera, including Cantor. Technically speaking he was neither a singer nor a dancer. It was the delivery and timing that did it. He had a feverish, infectious gaiety that swept across the footlights and carried everyone with it, and back of it was a kind of joyous tenderness that went to the heart. Also he wrote a lot of his own things which were, of course, an extension of the Cantor qualities. Ziegfeld often would suggest that Cantor write his own material, for here was something that was tied so deeply and inextricably to his personality that no one else could really do it. These were the qualities that Cantor carried with him into his successes in the movies, radio and TV. He carried them with him also into his philanthropic work.

I am not going to attempt to list all the things he has done; but over the years he has worked for the Red Cross, Cathedral of St. John the Divine in New York, Children Refugees, Army and Navy Relief, Hadassah, Catholic Charities, infantile paralysis (he originated the phrase "March of Dimes"), orphan institutes and those for the aged and the blind. On one occasion, after visiting Francis Cardinal Spellman, Archbishop of New York, the Cardinal remarked, "My son, we could use you in *our* church." Cantor has given himself and his efforts wherever they were merited. And when he spoke of Will Rogers being a great American he neglected through modesty to mention another – Eddie Cantor.

Cantor emerged from the dirty, teeming, claustrophobic Lower East Side. Will Rogers came from the clean, great, wind-swept reaches of Oologah, Indian Territory, that was to become Oklahoma. Yet, as I have said, they had much in common and the basis of their mutuality was a feeling of and for humanity. They shared, let us say, a simplicity of heart. Rogers had virtually no sense of money. He gave thousands to charity and other thousands to needy friends, and he became a millionaire almost in spite of himself. When he was working for Ziegfeld he used to carry in his pocket as many as a dozen uncashed weekly pay checks. He lived so frugally by nature, not by avarice, that he had no need of them and then one day he would remember and deposit them all at once. Never in his life did he keep any kind of an account of personal or business transactions. Someone asked him once how he and his wife, the former Betty Blake (like Cantor, Rogers loved only one woman and was true to her always), could possibly manage their affairs in such a slovenly fashion. "Why, it's easy," Rogers answered. "We just put a check in the bank and draw on it until it's gone."

As with Cantor, the road Rogers trudged to success was long and hard. In fact, with his innate modesty, hidden beneath a quip and a lazy smile, he never did really believe that he was a top star and there were numerous times when he considered leaving the theatre and settling down to a quiet, peaceful life in Claremore, Oklahoma. Indicative of this facet of his character is one of his remarks on the relative importance of luck and work. "It's the four-leaf clover that brings home the bacon," he said. Of Cherokee blood on his father's side (his mother was a devout Methodist who dreamed her son would become a minister), Rogers became a cowhand when he was fourteen, and there was wanderlust in his feet. His formal schooling was scanty. He attended high school irregularly and under silent protest at the urging of his father. He even had a bowing acquaintance with a military school for a while, but this was not for him either. Beyond the plains lay the great, mysterious outside world and Rogers was determined to see it. He did. Down south somewhere there was a place called Argentina, and the reports were that it was a paradise for cowboys. His father, who had given his son a herd of cattle, bought them back for $3,000, in the hope that when the money was gone the prodigal would return home to stay. The money went soon enough but the prodigal did not return, not for keeps anyway.

Characteristically, Will went to Argentina by way of London, after finding out the hard way that there was no boat service to Buenos Aires from New Orleans. He found Argentina a disastrous paradise. There was no need for American cowboys, rather a chilling lack of enthusiasm, and Rogers went broke in Buenos Aires after having spent or been swindled out of his poke. He got a job on a cattleboat for Durban, Africa, and was miserably seasick all the way. Rogers had heard there was a war going on (the Boer) and he hoped to find a little excitement in fighting in it. He arrived in its closing moments; in fact it ended just about the time he landed, and Rogers was broke and jobless once more in a strange and alien land. He got a job as a horse handyman on a ranch, quit it to drive mules to Ladysmith, and here fortune tapped him on the shoulder and said, "Son, I have been looking for you." Texas Jack's Wild West Circus was playing in Ladysmith, and Rogers, after a demonstration of his ability, got a job as a roper. He was billed as "The Cherokee Kid," a label he was to carry with him for years. After months with the Texas Jack show, Rogers became restless again and headed for Australia with a letter of recommendation in his pocket from Texas Jack to George Wirth, member of one of the great theatrical families down under. So Rogers toured Australia and New Zealand under the Wirth banner and presently, restless again, came back home for a brief visit by way of San Francisco.

But show business was in his blood now and soon he was off to St. Louis, where he joined a wild west show organized by Zach Mulhall. And that circuitously brought him on his first professional visit to New York, and

Madison Square Garden. That in turn led to vaudeville and, in truth, Will was pretty bad at first. He was talked out of quitting by Charley Mack of Moran and Mack and sweated it out. There was a girl and a pony in the act, which Rogers lassoed, and it was in this show, according to some historians — according to others it was when Rogers was at the Chicago Auditorium, you can take your pick — that he shyly let go his first witticism across the footlights. "Yep, spinnin' a rope's a lot of fun," he observed, "providin' your neck ain't in it." At any rate, after a swing through several vaudeville circuits Rogers reached Hammerstein's Roof in New York which, with the Palace, was then about as high as a variety actor could reasonably expect to go, and that was where Ziegfeld first saw him. He had dropped the pony and girl and other accessories. There was nothing really astonishing about Rogers' act — in fact when his Arkansas-born bride first saw it in Newark she was bored. It was the Rogers personality that put him over even then.

Ziegfeld acquired him for his Midnight Frolics, the fashionable and intimate late night show on the roof of the New Amsterdam, and although Rogers stayed with it through the run, not even Ziegfeld had any notion of the magnitude of the star. Rogers was all right for the intimate Frolics, but was he all right for the splendor of the Follies? Ziegfeld wondered and took a chance, but not before the Follies of 1917 was sagging badly and very clearly something new and fresh was needed. Rogers leaped at the chance without even asking "How much?" and went over with a smash. Thereafter he nightly played the Follies performance and then did his midnight stint in the Frolics. His style was the same. He had found his métier now, simple, humorous, homespun stuff that sometimes cut and sometimes was gentle but was never off-color. Once Rogers lassoed Fred Stone, who was sitting three rows back in the center, and pulled him on stage. He asked Stone about his wife and children and other personal matters as if he had happened to meet him on a sidewalk and was exchanging the time of day.

Ziegfeld almost never failed to catch a Rogers appearance, for the reason that he always said what happened to come into his head. "You know," Ziegfeld said once, "I'm not supposed to have a very quick sense of humor. Half the great comedians I've had in my shows that I paid a lot of money to and who made my customers shriek were not only not funny to me, but I couldn't understand why they seemed funny to anybody. But this Rogers, I never miss him if I can help it, though you'd be surprised how many of my expensive comics I've run out on and locked myself in my office when they were on stage." Rogers was among the rare few who ever kidded Ziegfeld and got away with it. At rehearsals Ziegfeld used to have a habit, when things were going wrong, of leaping from his chair in the darkness of the orchestra and screaming "Stop it! Stop it!" and of course, everything stopped. There were more than a few rehearsal times when Rogers used to sneak into the orchestra and do this imitation of Ziegfeld so perfectly that the cast was frozen into immobility by what they thought was the bark of the master's voice, and Ziegfeld himself joined in the ensuing laughter.

In the nearly ten years Rogers worked for Ziegfeld there was never a written contract between them. Ziegfeld tried it once and never tried again. Rogers looked at him and said, "I don't like contracts. You can trust me and I know I can trust you." A verbal gentleman's agreement did it, and it succeeded. When Rogers finally left the Follies to make movies in California, Ziegfeld presented Rogers with a watch engraved: *To Will Rogers, in appreciation of a great fellow, whose word is his bond.*

It is a sidelight on the relationship between these two that, while many of his intimates called Ziegfeld "Ziggy" or "Flo," to Rogers he was always "Mr. Ziegfeld." There was no coolness intended. It was merely a mark of admiration and respect. Rogers had some amusing things to say about Ziegfeld in later years, but none was unkind. "Ziegfeld," Rogers said, "took Michelangelo's statues, took some of the fat off them with a diet of lamb chops and pineapples, then he and a confederate named Ben Ali Haggin brought the statues to life, only with better figures, and the only marble about them was from the ears north." This last clause was a generalization that, one may surmise, Rogers did not really mean, except in instances when the marble was too obvious to be ignored, for the girls of the Follies in general adored him and he in return gave them the warmth of his kindness. Perhaps one reason for their adoration is that Rogers never made the slightest sexual move toward them. They were beautiful, they were desirable, but he had a wife and he loved her alone.

The rest of the Rogers career is, of course, inspiring Americana: his success in the talking movies (he flopped in the silents because his personality could not get across), his news commentaries, his radio fame, his habit of treating kings, presidents, and taxi drivers all the same, his interest in politics, polo and flying — the latter leading to his death in Alaska with Wiley Post in 1935 — the simplicity of his living and his stature as a philosopher-wit.

Some of the things he said are fresh and applicable today; for example, "Our foreign dealings are an open book, generally a checkbook." Another time he remarked, "I never hated anybody or anything." It was his own epitaph.

Rogers and W. C. Fields are related in time but not at all in temperament. They first met in what was the era of struggle for both of them, in Africa, where Fields was a juggler in Texas Jack's show. Later they worked for Ziegfeld over nearly the same span of years. There is no evidence that there ever was any friendship between them, merely the ties of association. Fields is considered by many to have been the Falstaff of his time, but actually he was only so in his enormous capacity for alcohol. Fields' announced cure for a hangover was the juice of three bottles of whiskey. Once when he was driving into Florida with companions and two cases of gin on the back seat they stopped to give a lift to a man trudging along the road. When the man identified himself as a minister on his way to give a temperance lecture, Fields physically pushed him out of the auto and ranted for the rest of the journey on the evils of temperance.

Fields was no Falstaff. He lacked gusto and he was deficient in humanity. Often he was cantankerous, rude, blindly egotistical and selfish, and his pinchpenny compulsions drove him to cache large sums of money under an unbelievable number of different names all over this country. Many believe there are untold thousands of dollars still stashed away in accounts that Fields forgot about. Yet, paradoxically, he was one of the funniest men of his era and an even greater paradox is the fact that there were many who loved him, knowing and expecting nothing in return.

In his case clearly the boy explains the man. He ran away from his Philadelphia home when he was eleven after a violent quarrel with his father. He slept in holes in the ground, in freight cars, anywhere that offered the suggestion of shelter; he stole milk and vegetables and connived with another boy to steal coins from Chinese laundrymen. He worked up a routine for obtaining free lunches in saloons by sitting at a table and ordering two plates of soup or bread and cheese, explaining that his father would be along in a minute or two. Needless to say, Daddy never arrived.

He set out to become a juggler after seeing one at a Philadelphia theatre. He worked with apples at first, and he worked very hard, up to eighteen hours a day. It has been asserted that it requires more practice to be a juggler than to be a pianist. Later some of his friends got him some steel balls to replace the apples. Fields never had a juggling lesson but whenever he could steal enough money from laundrymen he would go to see a professional, if one was in town.

Discomfort and hunger were the boy's daily companions but he never let them check his ambition. His first chance came at an amusement park at five dollars a week, then a real one came when Sliding Billy Watson, the burlesque comedian, who had met him and liked him, got him a job in Atlantic City at ten dollars a week. Fields found an old trunk in a refuse lot. Into it went the steel balls, a broken umbrella, and a battered high hat he had picked up somewhere. His was a tramp act, of course. It had to be. His clothes wouldn't permit anything else.

And so he was off. Since juggling is a "dumb act" requiring no language, only properties and pantomime, Fields in time took his act through most of Europe and into Africa and Australia. It was in this latter land that his first big break came. He received a cable in 1914 from Charles Dillingham to appear in this country in *Watch Your Step,* a revue featuring Vernon and Irene Castle. Fields made a thirty-eight-day trip to make the opening of

INTERNATIONAL NEWS PHOTOS, INC.

W. C. Fields and Ray Dooley in the Follies of 1925

the show at Rochester, New York, and was promptly dropped. "The juggler is out," was the verdict after the first night. But Gene Buck, lyricist and composer, who was scouting for Ziegfeld, promptly signed the juggler for the Follies and there began an association of ten years.

Fields got along well enough with other Ziegfeld comedians with the exception of fly-catchers. A fly-catcher is a comedian who uses no props at all. He gets his laughs by facial contortions and flashing movements of the fingers and hands, as if in catching flies. Fields on the other hand was completely dependent on properties: for example, in his celebrated billiard and golf acts; when a cuckoo bird laid an egg in his hat; or when, as a dentist, he released a canary from a patient's whiskers.

Fields had two fly-catcher enemies. One was Ed Wynn, the other Harry Kelly. The first year he appeared in the Follies was 1915, and one evening Fields discovered something was going wrong with his act. He was not getting laughs where there should have been laughs, and he was getting laughs where there shouldn't. Fields couldn't understand it until he looked under the billiard table and discovered Wynn there, fly-catching. "I'll kill him if he does it again," Fields told the management. For an interval there was peace. Then the Follies hit the road, and in Boston the laughing-in-the-wrong-place plague re-occurred. Once more Wynn was under the table. Fields slugged him on the head with his billiard cue and Wynn moaned and rolled over. The audience roared, thinking it part of the act.

Harry Kelly, who was a big Ziegfeld star, was assigned by the master, in a moment of sadism, to act as Fields' caddy in his golf scene. Kelly fly-catched the act away, and Fields slugged him off stage roaring, "Give me anybody, anybody but Kelly." He pointed at a stagehand, "Give me him." This was William Blanche, a dwarf with a huge head, who became the most famous of the Fields stooges.

There were a number of women in Fields' life. It has been estimated that each of his affairs, including that with his wife, lasted seven years, which may or may not appeal to the superstitious. His affair in the Follies, immediately following his separation from his wife, was with Bessie Pool. Bessie was in the opening number in "The Birth of Elation." In a way, it was. Bessie had long, lovely legs and was considered the best dancer in the chorus. One evening the juggler looked at her and smiled, and Bessie looked at him and smiled, and that was it. Thereafter it was taken for granted that Bessie was Fields' girl. Her dressing room was crowded with gifts from him, and they went riding together, each alternately taking the wheel in Fields' automobile. Thereafter Bessie had a baby and there was, naturally, a deal of speculation as to who was the sire. The matter never was cleared up completely, but in 1927 Fields made a cash settlement of $20,000 on Bessie and in return she signed an affidavit stating that W. C. Fields was not the father of her child.

The relations between Ziegfeld and Fields were those of a businessman with a valuable piece of property. Ziegfeld, as I have indicated, did not think highly of comedians other than Rogers. He tended to consider them merely fill-ins while the girls were changing for the next scene. At the close of a Fields' sketch at one rehearsal, Ziegfeld asked how long it took. Twenty-eight minutes, he was told. "How long does it take the girls to dress for the next scene?" Ziegfeld asked. Seven minutes, was the answer. "Cut the sketch to seven minutes," ordered Ziegfeld, and Fields never had a consummate admiration for him after that. In fact, it was not long afterward that Fields moved out of the Follies and into the domain of the movies, where he remained with increasing fame until his death on Christmas Day, 1946.

chapter five

"A Pretty Girl Is Like a Melody . . ." was written by Irving Berlin for the 1919 Follies but lived to become the theme song of Florenz Ziegfeld's sensational spectacles, and there are those today who never hear the hauntingly wistful tune without envisioning a woman of stately loveliness draped in chiffon and pearls, her long-legged beauty topped by a giant-size glittering headdress, moving slowly and beautifully across a stage or down a staircase. The Great Glorifier offered various explanations throughout the years of how he chose his girls, and probably the most revealing was this: "They must attract men. You cannot define the quality. In one word, I would say it was promise; a promise of romance and excitement – all the things a man dreams about when he thinks of the word *girl.* 'A pretty girl is like a melody that haunts you night and day'; that's it, that haunting quality. Some plain women have it, only when they have it they're not plain any more." And Ziegfeld recognized that the "haunting quality," that undefinable and illusive attribute, that promise of enchantment, whatever it was, made a Ziegfeld Girl.

Throughout the years some 3,000 girls were hand-picked by the master of allure, who needed only to see one walk across a stage to know instinctively – and instantly – whether she had that magical gift, a gift that brought millionaires, ambassadors and other male members of the VIP set from 1907 to 1931 to the front-row seats night after night.

Here are Ziegfeld's own ingredients for enchantment:

Figure: Bust 36 – waist 26 – hips 38. The accent was on hips. For

Famous Ziegfeld Girls of the Twenties

THE ZIEGFELD CLUB

perfection they should be always two inches larger than the bosom.

Nudity: He used the undraped figure only in Ben Ali Haggin tableaux. Then the nudes were scattered here and there among the laces, rosebuds and spangles of his fabulous settings. And never was a nude girl allowed to move as much as her little finger.

Allure: Bare legs were never as enticing as legs sheathed in the finest silk and chiffon, and tights were more seductive than nakedness. It was the art of intimation rather than disclosure.

Ziegfeld never lost the cool appraising touch of the connoisseur. He interviewed as many as 15,000 girls a year — girls from farms and factories, waitresses, models, office workers — any who were lucky enough to get past the stage-door man when the word was around that Ziegfeld was casting for a new show. To be labeled a Ziegfeld Girl was the dream of innumerable maidens and otherwise throughout all of America, and a goodly portion of the world. Their average salary was $75 a week but they wore ermines, sables, mink and diamonds. And if anyone gave a party for them — and some astonishing people did — they took for granted emeralds or at least thousand-dollar bills tucked into vanity cases as their just due.

But it wasn't only on stage that Ziegfeld was a hard taskmaster. He demanded they be well-groomed in the streets, hotels, restaurants or wherever they were seen by the public. In other words, Ziegfeld was their finishing school. He insisted upon gloves, hats, high heels and stockings at all times. One good suit, expensive and well tailored, was far more important than several cheap ones. A single evening dress, simply fashioned of fine material, was immensely more impressive than several changes of ill-fitting gowns of cheaper material. Too much rouge, mascara or lipstick off stage was as forbidden as wearing a costume with the slightest variation from his dictates. And woe to the girl who appeared at a rehearsal untidily or overly dressed. What girl would take a chance of losing her position as a member of the long-stemmed beauties that made up the most beautiful bouquet the world has ever known? Not one who had been fortunate enough to have heard the magic "You" in the high-pitched voice of Ziegfeld as he sat in the orchestra's first row center and scanned the hundreds of aspirants who walked across the brightly lighted barren stage at casting time. That *you* opened the gates to a legendary realm for the most famous girls the world has ever known.

But Ziegfeld, ever on the watch for the bewitchment of a beautiful body, a lovely face poised on a patrician neck, or a charm that was "haunting," always hunted through the restaurants, the streets, or wherever his days took him, a collector of beauty and a connoisseur of charm, for someone new to add to his gallery of the greatest beauties. He needed to look but once at the titian-haired, white-skinned Jessica Reed whom he saw in the Passing Show of 1918 to realize that regardless of the salary she demanded — and Jessica asked for and was paid the astounding salary for a showgirl of $125 — she had to adorn the next edition of the Follies.

He sent her a note backstage and Jessica threw it on the shelf without reading it; then, getting out of her scanty costume, she heard the stage-door man's voice announce, "There's a guy outside who wants to see you." Reluctantly she went to the door and, in her own words, "almost fainted" when she recognized Ziegfeld and heard him say, "I want you for my show." Jessica made her debut walking on stage as John Steel sang "A Pretty Girl Is Like a Melody," doing nothing more than stand with four other beauties as the audience clapped their appreciation for Steel, the music and the pretty girls. But Jessica was more than pretty — she was truly beautiful, with perfect features, magnificent coloring and a statuesque body. It was a beauty that was to lead to five husbands, the squandering of a million dollars, and finally to a lonely and penniless death in a hospital ward under the title of "Bad Luck's Baby."

A natural-born showgirl, she was so beautiful that as one critic put it "she could have chewed tobacco on stage and it would have seemed charming." She was born Jessie Rogers near Houston, Texas. Necessity forced her to leave elementary school at a time when most of her playmates were fondling dolls and floundering toward high school. Young Jessie went to work in a cracker factory and left there when she saw a waitress-wanted sign in a hash-house in Houston. It was there she met her first husband, Oliver Debrow, a black-face comedian of a one-night-stand company. Jessie waited on him and he won her heart by his funny talk and his promise of a small part for her in his barnstorming company. Both the comedian and his child bride — Jessie was fifteen — thought he was doing her a tremendous favor when he put her on the payroll at seven dollars a week. Immature of face and figure though she was, the company had accidentally picked up a bargain. Jessie's young beauty was more than appreciated by the Southwest's male audiences.

The first marriage, like all the others, ended in divorce, but it brought about two of the most important events in her life — the birth of her only child, a daughter, Ann Carroll Debrow, and her chance to get on the stage. The comedian in Debrow turned to tragedian when he won a divorce and custody of the child on evidence which the court saw fit to seal, for he had killed Leslie Nash on Jessie's account and successfully eluded the murder charge by pleading "the unwritten law." Jessie left for New York alone. She described years later the lure of the big city and the lights of the theatre: "I was born to drink water, but having tasted champagne I wanted to taste it again." As she boarded the New York-bound train even Jessie herself couldn't have dreamed where the pathetic little "taste of champagne" was to lead.

In New York, while other girls only slightly less lovely went from agent to agent until their hearts and their pocketbooks were broken, Jessie walked right into the chorus of the Passing Show of 1918. It was then that she married her second husband, Louis Herzberg, but that soon ended in divorce too. When she joined the Follies she rose to be among the four topmost beauties of the postwar period. Ziegfeld himself placed her slightly below Peggy Hopkins Joyce and on a par with Jean Nash, who became an international celebrity famous for her jewels and charm. It seemed that the red-haired, Texas-born beauty had passed her streak of misfortune. But fate had more – much, much more – in store for poor little Jessie Rogers who was the toast of Broadway as Jessica Reed.

Jessica's fame rose as her beauty grew – and it grew the way a bruised bud grows into a full-blown flower. Her nourishment was adulation and money. She soon earned the title of the highest-paid show girl on Broadway, which at that time was synonymous with the world. Ziegfeld was paying her $250 a week and Jessica was spending it on furs, jewels, clothes, automobiles and trips to Florida and California. She learned what real champagne was like, the taste of caviar, and went on rounds and rounds of parties, wondering sometimes in her gaiety what the bill was but never wondering long enough to let it bother her. Somehow bills always got paid and what was money for but to be spent? She pretended to care nothing for tomorrow – it was always today for Jessica – and she certainly acted up to her philosophy. Men fell in love with her at first sight and seemed unable to resist her even when she herself showed not the slightest interest.

Jessie Reed, the highest-paid chorus girl in the world.

INTERNATIONAL NEWS PHOTOS, INC.

THE ZIEGFELD CLUB

Jessie Reed in her famous "Lace Number"

Her third marriage was to young Dan Caswell, the scion of a wealthy Cleveland family, who, hardly old enough to vote, met her on a train en route from New York to Boston while he was pleasantly speculating on how he would spend a quarter of a million dollars he had just inherited. As the train pulled out of the darkened tunnel of Grand Central Station he watched fascinated as a girl with flaming hair walked down the aisle, the train's motion forcing her slim figure into alluring movements. Young Caswell wanted to leave his seat right then and there and ask her to marry him but knew it would only make him seem ridiculous. There didn't seem any way to keep this vision of loveliness from passing into the next car and out of his life until, to his infinite joy, with a swish of her skirts and a faint breath of perfume she slipped into the seat opposite him. Later, after she and his quarter-million had both been removed from his life, the young millionaire enjoyed telling about the one moment he was never to forget: "When I met Jessie on that train."

Not until they reached Boston and he followed her by taxi to the same hotel did he learn that she was Jessica Reed of the Follies. Jessica had been carrying a box of chocolates and a mauve-colored volume of poems and he was convinced that she was a proper young Bostonian returning to school after a week end in New York. He hadn't dared speak to her and had wracked his brains all the way to Boston for some proper way of being introduced. Two years later, at the time of their divorce, he said with bitterness, "People tell me Jessie wasn't an actress. Maybe not on stage but I can give them an off stage testimonial. By avoiding every sign of a flirtation she hooked me with consummate skill." What Jessica felt about the young man, if she felt anything, has never been printed. But the year was 1921 and Follies girls took wining and dining as a matter of course and looked upon hundred-dollar bills about as indifferently as a Pullman porter would regard a ten-cent tip.

That night in the lobby of the Boston hotel Caswell called all the Follies beauties down to the lobby and with a gesture that he hoped reeked of sophistication but which actually was pathetically young, he opened a chamois bag of diamonds that belonged to his mother — diamonds worth $30,000 — and sprinkled them over the marble floor. An instant later the floor was covered with scrambling girls, pulling, pushing and grabbing. It was at that moment that he asked the titian-haired beauty to marry him, and pausing only to remove the diamond from her mouth where she'd put it for self-keeping, she softly murmured "Yes."

How did he happen to have this bag of diamonds? you may ask. There is a touch of impetuous irony here and a bagful of pathos, too. Caswell was the son of D. O. Caswell and the godson of President McKinley. His mother was a distinguished society leader, and when she saw her son off to Boston she did so with calm and patrician expectations for his future. He was engaged to a popular Boston debutante of that year and the diamonds he scattered on the lobby floor were family heirlooms intended to be made into a necklace for his fiancée.

Casually, Caswell next pulled a $12,000 diamond ring out of his pocket, also belonging to his mother and intended for his fiancée, and placed it on Jessica's engagement finger. That evening he watched the Follies anxiously, waiting and hoping the lovely Jessica wouldn't have a change of heart. She didn't. They were married before next day's matinee. He was alone with his bride in their suite when the reporters and photographers barged in, and through their questions Dan Caswell learned that not only had Jessica been married before but that there was a child and there had been a shooting.

Jessica dissolved into tears. Many more tears were to fall and many more reconciliations took place with more jewels, furs and cars as measures of appeasement. Caswell announced after Jessica had divorced him that those few months cost him his entire fortune. He died at twenty-five, having come into another $250,000 which did not go to Jessica. Nor did any of the money he had given her stick to her bank account any longer than a snowflake to her ermine and mink coats. But she always had her salary, had it, that is, for the short time it took her to spend it.

Her next two husbands were William F. Young, a Chicago advertising man, and Leonard Reno, a World War flier, the son of an extremely wealthy publisher. He proved to be a financial misfortune because his father had heard all about his daughter-in-law's careless ways with money and kept them on a strict allowance. Jessica seems to have liked Reno best because she stayed with him four years, the longest any of her marriages had lasted. All in all, she seems to have thought men treated her shabbily, for toward the end of her life she remarked, "Remember, for every heart on Broadway, there are two heels." This was indeed an aphorism of self-pity.

This girl who was the quintessence of loveliness, feted, courted and given a fortune in jewels, died penniless in Chicago's Osteopathic Hospital where she had gone with a streptococcic infection and a leaky heart due to her many years of drinking. She was forty-three and gone were her diamonds, her five husbands, and every bit of the million dollars she estimated she had spent in her brief and dazzling years of gaiety. She had been on relief twice, it was rumored, and she left to her daughter: "A million dollars' worth of face and figure and what more could any girl want?" Jessica went to meet the tomorrow she had lived for alone as she took her final curtain call without any applause. She was "hard luck's baby," but her basic hard luck was in herself.

Like Jessica Reed, in fact like so many of the Ziegfeld girls, was little Olive Thomas, whose loveliness carried her from a drab, dreary childhood of poverty to fame and fortune, to what seemed the dreams she cherished for happiness, and on to a young, pathetically young, death in Paris, where either by intent, design or perhaps accidentally — it has never been determined — she swallowed bichloride of mercury after a round of the little cafés in Montmartre. Olive had come a long way to reach Paris, a part of the world she had known about only from her geography books. In 1912, when she was selling gingham by the yard behind the counter in Horne's emporium in McKees Rocks, a small town outside of Pittsburgh, she dreamed of Broadway. Yet her dreams, once they began to materialize, carried her almost on a legendary magic carpet to Ziegfeld. Harrison Fisher, the noted artist, said of her Follies debut: "Beauty is not one feature or quality but the sum of them all. Olive Thomas has that sum in an amazingly high degree."

Olive Thomas PICTURE COLLECTION, NEW YORK PUBLIC LIBRARY

Olive loathed the dingy gloom of McKees Rocks, the endless line of smokestacks, the high-stooped narrow houses that lined the streets bearing the grime of laboring Pittsburgh, the belching smoke that rose above blackened sheet-iron mills. Little is known of the early childhood of Olive Elaine Duffy, who was born October 16, 1898, in Charleroi, Pennsylvania, the second of three children of Mr. and Mrs. James Duffy. Her father was a structural steel worker. Upon his death the burden of caring for young Olive and her two brothers, James and William, fell upon Mrs. Duffy, who went to work by the day to support her family. Olive had only the barest of schooling, little opportunity to play, and lacked even the shoes and dresses such as the children of ordinary workers had.

When she was ten, her mother, who by then was operating a restaurant, met and married Harry M. Van Kirk, a railroad conductor. The family moved to McKees Rocks and as Olive Van Kirk the startlingly beautiful child went to the Blaine Public School and yearned to grow up fast so that she could get away to a life that meant a pretty dress now and then and meals that weren't comprised of oatmeal, fried potatoes and sometimes a box of stale cookies as a treat. When she was fourteen she dressed her hair high on her head like a girl of twenty. Her friends, acquaintances really, for Olive never knew anyone intimately in those days, were all older than she. By the time she put her hair up she was selling in Horne's at what was to her the fabulous salary of three dollars a week. But more than the money she made (most of which she had to contribute to keep the household in bare necessities), her job brought to her a Prince Charming in the form of Bernard Krug Thomas, a hard-working businessman. They were married and went to live with the Thomas family on a street and in a house that was little different from what she had always known. This was one of her first disappointments, for she found that her marriage did not bring her appreciably nearer her ideal of a happy and luxurious life.

How could she escape from her drab surroundings into the brighter life she knew existed somewhere? That was the question that insistently gnawed at her. After two years of marriage she left Thomas and returned to her mother's home, despondent but determined and fiercely hungry. She was now eighteen, with an ethereal beauty, and she was not going to waste that beauty in a town where even the clothes hung out on the line to dry were gray with smoke, the color of the gloom that surrounded her. With another girl she went to work in Pittsburgh as a model in a fashion show in Kaufman's department store. The show lasted only a week but Olive had had her taste of glamor, the feel of silk against her young body, and having had it she wanted more and more.

The next step was New York, the city she'd read about, where many poor girls had become actresses, singers and movie stars. And hadn't she seen the pictures of Ziegfeld girls that had excited the admiration of the young men around grimy McKees Rocks? Olive looked at herself critically and knew that she was as pretty — if not prettier — than the girls in the Follies or on the pastel-tinted candy boxes she saw in the drugstore window. On borrowed money she came to New York during the winter of 1913 and supported herself by posing for photographers and artists until she managed to get in to see Ziegfeld several months later. He recognized her beauty in a flash of understanding and hired her when he auditioned hundreds of girls for his 1914 Follies. Almost from the moment she stepped on the stage

Olive was quickly acknowledged by the front-row connoisseurs as breath-taking.

She went back to McKees Rocks on February 25, 1915, long enough to be granted an uncontested divorce from her husband, whom she charged with cruelty and neglect. She returned there only once more, in July 1919, to attend the funeral of her brother James' wife. It was the last link she had with her penniless childhood and the misery of squalor. A hundred-dollar check sent weekly to her mother made out in Olive's childish, almost un-formed writing, and now and then an inappropriate present — a lace negli-gee, the sheerest of silk stockings, luxuries to be neither worn nor bought in McKees Rocks — these were her only reminders of a part of her life she so desperately wanted to forget.

She was seen as "Miss New York" in her first Follies appearance and she was earning the usual Follies salary of $75 a week. But Olive had relent-less ambition as well as wide brown eyes with an appealing quality of sad-ness, a wealth of soft brownish hair, a complexion that needed little if any make-up, and a delicately formed body. Dreams and determination were the fuse for the meteoric success of Olive Elaine Duffy, who became Olive Thomas, the courted favorite of Broadway.

When she left the stage to go to Hollywood she was making $2,500 a week and, if for no other reason than to watch her parade as a vision of desire, she earned every bit of it. But even this did not meet her insatiable expectations. She found that she was far from rich enough to command all the luxuries enjoyed by the more fortunate members of the circle in which she moved. She had to depend on others, men whose names meant power and prestige, a few women friends who had married into socially prominent families or whose husbands were wealthy. This necessity was galling to her. That and that alone is what took Olive from the stage she loved to the strange land of Hollywood and the silent movies.

The year was 1917 and Olive had had three years of adoration on Broad-way. Ziegfeld called her the embodiment of perfect loveliness, millionaire playboys and elderly capitalists were besieging her with offers of marriage, and Olive, her heart still that of a small-town girl, was waiting for the Knight on a White Charger to sweep her off her feet. He came, or at least the little girl from McKees Rocks was certain he had arrived, when she was introduced to suave, handsome, twenty-year-old Jack Pickford. He was the brother of "America's Sweetheart," as Mary Pickford with her long golden curls and pouting mouth was known throughout the world. Even to calloused Broad-way it was love at first sight, a puppy love, for Olive was a year younger than the youthful Pickford. It was an ardent devotion from their third meeting, when Jack gave Olive a diamond and platinum cigarette case valued at $12,000 and inscribed: *To Olive Thomas — the only sweetheart I will ever have.* Members of the Pickford family, mainly Jack's mother,

INTERNATIONAL NEWS PHOTOS, INC.

Jack Pickford and his wife Olive Thomas

objected to the match and begged the young couple to wait, think it over, get to know each other — all the clichés with which families have cautioned their children since days beyond recall.

They were married, nevertheless, within a few months of their meeting and the first quarrel came shortly after their honeymoon. It was patched up quickly but later clashes in temperament led to separations and reconciliations. Olive was making great strides in silent films and earning more money than she ever had dared hope for. She became one of the most popular ingenues on what was called the silver screen — innocent, childish, lovable and always beautiful — and she even began to rival, in the minds of many, the fantastic success of her sister-in-law. But there was something lacking in her life; happiness was still an elusive quality. It might have been due to the influence of a tremendous income on a girl reared in poverty and still unprepared to accept the fact that life isn't all romance. Jack Pickford, after a serious break in 1920, made it up again with her and decided postwar Paris was the paradise for their second honeymoon. This was another of Olive's dreams — a chance to see wicked, wonderful Paris with all the money necessary to enjoy its delights and with an escort who was rich, handsome, and her husband.

They must have both tried to recapture the love or infatuation, call it what you will, they had felt for one another at their first meeting. A letter upon their arrival stated that they were enjoying "an unbelievably happy honeymoon." Then there was silence. According to one report, Olive, brokenhearted, was convinced that she could never live with her husband again. Jack made a hurried trip from Paris to London and when he rejoined his wife, Olive told him, or so a friend's letter read, that further life with him would be impossible and abhorrent. Perhaps wishing to forget her sorrows and reckless of all other considerations Olive started out one Saturday night to "live" Paris as only a desperate, sorrowing young girl, never emotionally adult, could imagine it should be lived.

After a dinner at which she did little more than toy with her food and drink an abundance of champagne she left for a tour of Montmartre, fiercely gay, singing, drinking as if she had but one night to live. As dawn was breaking over the Sacré Coeur basilica, which would be filled with worshipers in a scant few hours, Olive returned to their apartment in the Ritz. Her nerves frayed from her night of excitement and her despair, she recklessly and probably mistaking them for sleeping medicine, poured into her slim hand a number of bichloride tablets. Filling a glass from the silver-plated faucet, she popped them into her mouth. They didn't bring the sleep she craved or the oblivion she probably wanted more than anything else in the world at that moment; they brought instead an agony not obliterated until her death four days later. A doctor from the American Hospital in Neuilly was hastily summoned by Jack Pickford when he heard Olive's screams and found her on the bathroom floor. With a McKees Rocks outlook on life, Olive said to the doctor merely: "Well, doctor, Paris has got me."

A police announcement several days after her death showed that they were in considerable doubt as to why an intelligent woman could make the mistake of taking poison instead of the sleeping pills she was accustomed to, but they were unable to find that it was anything but an accident. She died on a beautiful September morning in 1920. Her death remains shrouded in mystery, a mystery that went to the grave with the still-childlike beauty of her face and her slim lovely figure.

After a thorough investigation by the French police the body of Olive

Thomas was shipped home on board the *Mauretania,* accompanied by her husband in deepest mourning. He was plainly on the verge of breakdown and wept openly when speaking to reporters in broken, halting words of his wife's death. "She did not want to die. We tried so hard to save her. We had no quarrels," was all the young Pickford could say over and over again. Her two brothers and her mother, Mrs. Harry Van Kirk, then living in Philadelphia, joined the sad little procession that followed the handsome metal coffin to the undertaking establishment. A day or so later services for the young girl from McKees Rocks were held at St. Thomas' Episcopal Church on Fifth Avenue, where an estimated 4,000 socialites, film stars, managers, directors and people who had known little Ollie from her early Ziegfeld days jammed the church. The crush was so great that women fainted and ushers and police attempted in vain to hold back the crowd.

When Olive's estate was settled, society leaders, stars of stage and screen and jewelry dealers met on equal ground to bid on the baubles — if you can call diamonds, town cars and furs baubles — that went under the auctioneer's hammer. Spirited bidding began when the auctioneer held up two gifts from Jack Pickford. One was the famous cigarette case and the other a gold toilet set which went to Mable Normand, a film star of those days, whose tenacity cost her $1,425. A necklace containing 310 pearls was bought by Mrs. Jerome Bonaparte. A sable coat went for $1,800, a town car for $5,000, and dealers purchased such items as a diamond and sapphire bracelet at $3,100, pearls worth $1,000 and so it went. Poor little Olive! She died owning everything in the world she had craved when she was behind the gingham counter — except happiness.

Pickford's charm continued to fascinate women but forgetfulness of Olive didn't come until two years later when he met Marilyn Miller, who was then starring in Ziegfeld's musical, *Sunny,* and was the toast of Broadway. It was ordained, perhaps, that they should be drawn together by the common bond of grief and lost love. In 1918, when she was twenty, she met and loved Frank Carter, a husky, handsome actor who died in a tragic automobile accident a few years after their marriage. In 1922 Jack and Marilyn were married at the home of Mary Pickford and Douglas Fairbanks in Hollywood. But, just as in the case of Olive, they quarreled and made up constantly until Marilyn divorced him in Paris in 1927 on grounds of desertion and neglect. Three years later he met Mary Mulhern, another of Ziegfeld's show girls although far from the big-name status of his two former wives, but she too divorced him in 1930. Never strong physically and with only a fair amount of success as a leading man in the movies, the pace he had tried to follow began to take its toll. It was fitting that Paris should be the setting for the last scene in his hectic life; wasn't it there that he had lost the two most sought-after women of the times? He died October 15, 1932 of multiple neuritis, in the same American hospital where lovely Olive had died.

chapter six

A stroke of rare good luck came into Ziegfeld's life — professionally speaking — and it was somewhat by chance and somewhat by being reluctantly led or actually pushed into the line of fortune's fire. Ziegfeld, like many men and perhaps more than most because his business was beauty, found nothing duller than spending an afternoon at a fashion showing. But finally one day at the insistence of Billie Burke he donned his black mink-lined coat and an air of martyrdom and accompanied his wife to Lady Duff-Gordon's salon, known as Lucile, Ltd., where the temperamental but sensational dress-maker was showing her latest collections. Miss Burke ordered one or two gowns that seemed to bring out the lovely lights in her red-gold hair and in which she was later to cause the turning of many heads as she swept into Delmonico's or the old Waldorf-Astoria; her husband, as husbands are prone to do, sat there politely but uncomfortably in a fragile gold chair, stifling yawns and looking longingly at his watch every few minutes.

But that all stopped when a tall girl, her yellow corn-silk hair piled on top of her head, moved with patrician posture across the salon. There followed more girls, lovely creatures who wore their gowns with an enormous amount of distinction, but Ziegfeld didn't see them really, or if he did he saw them only as a background for the statuesque, stately model. He looked at her again and again, never taking his eyes away from her graceful movements. He noted the way the silk folds of her dress clung to a body that was breath-takingly beautiful in motion. He was on the edge of his chair now and Miss Burke, wise to the ways of her husband, sat back in her chair, on her lips a soft smile that her husband was too intent to notice. The model was Dolores, an English girl who was to become perhaps the most spectacular beauty ever to appear in the Follies. So fascinated was Ziegfeld by the entire routine that he put Dolores in the 1917 version and reproduced what he had seen that day as "Ladies of Fashion," an "Episode of Chiffon" with gowns created by Lady Duff-Gordon and models including Peggy Hopkins Joyce and Lilyan Tashman among the nine in the number. But it was Dolores, the Empress of Fashion, playing "The Discourager of Hesitancy" who had all Broadway talking after that opening night on June 12, 1917.

Unlike most of his glorified girls Dolores came to Ziegfeld already well tutored in the art of charm and enchantment. He wasn't her finishing school. It was Lady Duff-Gordon who had put Dolores through her paces. It was she who had taught her to walk and speak correctly and carry her head proudly and haughtily. And Dolores learned quickly and capably under the strict tutelage of Lady Duff-Gordon, who was much pleased with her handiwork. She had a right to be, for Dolores, who was born Kathleen Rose of commonplace English parents, was working as an errand girl in her London salon about a year before Lady Duff-Gordon saw her and started training her, training her to bring out the beauty that was hers but which was hidden underneath poor posture and even poorer clothes. It began quite by chance one day when Lady Duff-Gordon was sitting regally in her office and Dolores fetched her mail. Lady Duff-Gordon paid no attention to her letters but stared and stared at the embarrassed girl.

"Heavens," she said at last in her very British voice, "what exquisite hair! But of course, my dear, you haven't the faintest idea how to wear it. Sit down there," she ordered. When she loosened the hairpins, a mist of shiny, baby-soft hair fell over the girl's young shoulders and with a few twists and a few more pins from her own hair she ordered, "Now look at yourself." Kathleen Rose stared at her reflection incredulously. The contours of her face seemed more delicate, there was a subtle change in her eyes, and the great masses of silky hair had been artfully arranged to bring out the gold to an astonishing degree. Lady Duff-Gordon was pleased and permitted an expression of honest admiration to cross her aristocratic features. "I think you are going to be a great beauty," she said. "No, I'm *sure* you will be if you will do as I say. Take off your clothes, Kathleen."

Kathleen Rose knew by this time the caprices of the temperamental lady who was her boss, so without a moment's hesitation she did as she was told, a little ashamed perhaps, but with a feeling Cinderella might have had when the fairy godmother waved her magic wand. And magic it was, too, when Lady Duff-Gordon rang for a bolt of exquisitely beautiful silk and, stuffing several pins into her mouth, in about five minutes draped and pinned a ravishing dress on the girl who was later to wear many of Ziegfeld's most radiant costumes. Pleased with her Pygmalion-like work, she told her secre-

THE ZIEGFELD CLUB

Dolores

THE ZIEGFELD CLUB

Dolores

tary she didn't want to be disturbed for an hour. "If anyone insists on seeing me, tell them I am doing the most important job in the world — I am creating beauty and cannot be bothered." Then she commanded Kathleen to walk and the frightened but happy girl walked. "Dreadful!" said Lady Duff-Gordon. "Awful! But just what I expected." She took half a dozen books and piled them, one on top of the other, on Kathleen's head. "Now when you've learned to walk without dropping any of these books you will have begun to carry yourself as the Lord intended," said the impetuous lady. "We'll practice for a half hour or so." For an hour Kathleen tried, until Lady Duff-Gordon stopped her. "Now let me see you walk without them," she said, and after nodding her head in approval, "What's your name?"

"Kathleen, madame," answered the girl.

"I don't like it," said Lady Duff-Gordon. "You look Spanish; you look like a blonde Spanish girl. You look as though you were capable of real experience. I don't suppose you really are, but you look so. Keep on looking so. Your name from now on will be Dolores!" And so was created Dolores, most beautiful of models, most perfect of Follies girls, with the poise of a duchess and the grace of poetry. But the transformation wasn't effected overnight. Day after day, for an hour every morning, Dolores walked up and down before Lady Duff-Gordon with books piled on her head and big jars held under her arms. The temperamental designer was unsparing in her criticism. After a year of this training Dolores knew how to walk, how to sit, how to stand faultlessly and beautifully. At the same time she was taught to speak in low, musical, well-bred tones with perfect English intonation and accent.

"The whole effect of a dress," Lady Duff-Gordon told her apt pupil, "can be spoiled by a harsh or unmusical note. My dresses, Dolores, would do honor to a duchess. I have taught you to behave like a duchess, and to carry yourself like one. The dress and you are in harmony. Together they delight and lull the customer. But suppose you answer a question and your voice is harsh, uncultured and disagreeable? The harmonies are broken! The dress perhaps is not sold — but worse, far worse than that, you have destroyed a thing of beauty!

"Always remember," she said, "that if you are good-looking and have a pleasant voice, it does not matter whether what you have to say makes any sense whatsoever. The eye is pleased with your beauty, the ear is pleased with your voice. And when one's eyes and ears are pleased and completely happy, it becomes annoying, actually distracting, to have to give any thought to what one is saying. If a girl is beautiful and her voice lovely, she does better to ripple along lightly, choosing words rather than sentences filled with ideas. Especially if she is vis-a-vis with a man."

After she had schooled Dolores and graciously handed her what would amount to her diploma — "You've learned well," she said — she had one more bit of advice, advice that a worldly-wise mother might give to her daughter as she took her place in the receiving line at her debut. And indeed, it was Dolores' coming-out party. "Be sure to make a good marriage. There isn't a home in England, much less in all of America, where you could not perfectly enact the chatelaine. There are many duchesses, my dear, who would give their right hands to have your poise, your grace, your carriage. No man need ever be ashamed of you. So be wise and marry well." That is how it was that Dolores served her apprenticeship and came to New York with the Duff-Gordon entourage and to a meeting with Florenz Ziegfeld.

Dolores was in one Ziegfeld show after another and toured for more than three years with the smash success *Sally,* in which Marilyn Miller and Leon Errol were starred. But today she is best remembered as the Peacock Girl who walked across the New Amsterdam Theatre Roof at midnight, proudly and haughtily, in one of the loveliest costumes ever seen on Broadway. It was in the Ziegfeld Midnight Frolics that Dolores wore the truly magnificent birdlike outfit that is reported to have cost well up in the thousands. Ziegfeld had it made in Paris and the oh's and ah's it drew when Dolores, her enticing figure draped in a pearl-trimmed white satin sheath, walked slowly on stage were as pleasing to the showman as though the ceiling had burst into a shower of diamonds. The effect as Dolores moved in the spotlight, the only light in the darkened room, was somewhat the same, actually. For towering well over the tall beauty's head and surrounding her slim body was a fan so enormous that it seemed likely to waft her from the boards. Her arms outstretched, she moved like a queen as the lights caught the glittering blue, green and pink paillettes and bugle beads that were embroidered to resemble the peacock's feathers on a white satin foundation. On her head was a white satin cap tied under her chin, and from the satin that covered her forehead erupted a glittering arrangement of peacock feathers. Her shoulders and arms were bare and it was from that night on that Dolores was called "the loveliest show girl in the world." Artists stressed the delicacy of her nose, mouth and chin, and there were geometrical analyses of her "perfect face," showing the flawless symmetry of her features.

An incorrect impression grew up about Dolores from those who did not know her well. This was that she was a mere mannequin, a clotheshorse, completely without personality. This is far from the truth. Off stage in the presence of friends she was lively and gay. On one occasion, during a period of rehearsals, Dolores attended a luncheon and found herself so pleasantly involved in champagne and chatter that the hours slipped by. Back at the theatre Ziegfeld first became annoyed — the great man was not accustomed to being treated thus — and then alarmed. He finally tracked her down and sent a courier with the imperious demand that Dolores return instantly.

Dolores airily waved the courier away. Finally she condescended to make her departure and arrived at the theatre with a case of champagne which, instead of trying to hide, she asked Ziegfeld to keep for her, please. He was so taken back by this regal affrontery that he never said a word. The rehearsal proceeded as though nothing had happened.

It was early in May, 1923, that Dolores boarded the *Olympic* for what ostensibly was to be nothing more than a European vacation, but what was in reality to become the longest role in her life. Her many trunks were filled with magnificent ball gowns and exquisite lingerie, and she posed on shipboard before sailing time looking radiantly happy in a gray suit which came down to her ankles and a gray hat trimmed with flowers the color of the

THE ZIEGFELD CLUB

Dolores in her Butterfly costume

pink in her cheeks. Her destination — and her destiny too — turned out to be Paris, for she was married there on May 15th to Tudor Wilkinson, an American sportsman and art patron. The marriage took place in the *mairie* of the First Arrondissement and afterward at the Oratoire du Louvre, with Mr. and Mrs. Dudley Field Malone as the only witnesses. Asked what their plans were, Mr. Wilkinson said, "There will be no honeymoon in the ordinary sense of the word. We hope the whole of our lives will be one long honeymoon." And it seems to have been so.

Dolores (whom Wilkinson always called Kathleen) had been in love with the American multimillionaire ever since they were introduced shortly after she became a sensation (to put it mildly) in the Follies. Night after night he sat in a third row center seat watching her as he might look at and adore a lovely piece from his fabulous collection of antiques or his Joshua Reynolds portraits. Originally from St. Louis, Wilkinson had lived in Europe for many years and it was to his Paris apartment — a suite occupying three floors and filled with priceless works of art — that he took his lovely bride. Surrounded by Gothic tapestries and rare needlepoint, the rooms fairly drenched in Renaissance atmosphere, Dolores in real life enacted the chatelaine as perfectly as Lady Duff-Gordon had predicted. But there was another prediction, this one made by Ziegfeld the day she sailed from America, and he was as wrong as Lady Duff-Gordon was right. "You will come back someday," he told her, which proved to be no more than wishful thinking on his part. "They always do." But Dolores never did. In an interview from Paris in 1935 she said in the same British accent which Leon Errol loved to mimic in the Follies, "I have simply made marriage and our home my career. I never enjoyed any success as much as I enjoy being an efficient housewife." So the girl who burst like a blinding jewel on Broadway was content inside a residential jewel box where her husband enshrined what he later called "the rarest gem in my collection — my wife."

A sordid pitiful antithesis, a tragic counterpoint to the true love and happiness of Dolores, runs like a sad and maudlin melody through the life of Imogene Wilson. Called "the most beautiful blonde on Broadway" when she was dazzling the Follies audiences in ermine-trimmed gowns, Ziegfeld's spectacular headdresses and strands of pearls draped over and around her slim body, unhappiness was her constant accompaniment. Almost from the day she was born she lived with it in the form of loneliness, scandal, lawsuits, bankruptcy, and above all a hopeless love for Frank Tinney, the black-faced comedian, a love that finally and inevitably was to wreck both their careers and, more important, their lives.

The first of the tragic events in her life began a few months after her birth in Louisville, Kentucky, on December 18, 1902, when both her parents died. It was then that she was placed in an orphanage — years later she was to refer to it as a convent — in St. Joseph, Missouri. The nuns who brought her up often remarked she had the face of an angel, but with red hair. Apparently there is no authentic record of a red-haired angel. As soon as she came to New York (it was in 1919) she corrected that discrepancy by bleaching her hair so that she finally did acquire an angelic countenance. It was that same wide-eyed, almost childish expression in her beautiful eyes that caused James Montgomery Flagg to use her over and over again as a model. She posed for other prominent artists too, but it was one of Flagg's canvases that Ziegfeld saw. It induced him to put her in the Follies. Imogene wore her wisps of lace, her sheaths of gold lamé and the beautiful but incredible headdresses magnificently, but unfortunately she also wore her heart on her sleeve from the moment she saw Frank Tinney in the New Amsterdam Theatre wings.

She often glanced in awe at the great comedian whom Ziegfeld was paying as much in one week as she could hope to receive in one season. One day Tinney noticed the beautiful "Bubbles" (a name carried over from her childhood) and offered to take her home in a taxi. It was the beginning of a famous or infamous relationship. Imogene was so flattered that she didn't bother to find out that Tinney was married, and he neglected to tell her. Later when taxed with this neglect he said, "Sure I have a wife, a mortgage and an appendix, but why should I bring these things up and spoil a pleasant evening? I believe a man should keep his troubles to himself." Imogene learned that he had a son, too. Then, instead of keeping her misfortune from the world, she told it on page one of the newspapers, pursued Tinney into his dressing room and to his home in Baldwin, Long Island, where she confronted his wife with the story of their love which, while not exactly in the Romeo-and-Juliet tradition, was nevertheless to be the only love in her entire life. The comedian grew awfully weary of this little eighteen-year-old girl who couldn't take a joke and soon she had some new complaints, a black-and-blue body as well as a badly bruised heart. In the Follies dressing rooms she exhibited an enormous black-and-blue spot on her stomach, acquired, she told the other beauties, from one of Tinney's not so funny feet. Their answer, or so it has been reported, was simple and direct: "Quiet! You little fool! What a husband doesn't know about a girl won't hurt her, but every millionaire in the country will know about you and Tinney and not one of them will marry you. If you keep this up you'll lose your job."

But Imogene continued to love blindly if not wisely until, like a badly beaten fighter leaving the ring, she obtained a warrant for the arrest of her slightly sadistic lover on a felonious-assault charge. She charged Tinney had entered her apartment on West 72nd Street in the small hours of the morning and attacked her, inflicting severe injuries, injuries that caused Dr. Jerome Wagner, Ziegfeld's personal physician, to observe: "This girl looks as though she had been struck by an automobile." Tinney languished several hours in a cell and then was brought face to face with his fair accuser in a courtroom. She was asking for $100,000 as damages. The suit made good reading for the subway straphangers and those whose only straphanging consisted of the velvet cord that made getting out of their Rolls easier.

Ziegfeld issued one rather terse statement in the press which read:

> I believe this little girl is an innocent victim. Her place in the 1924 edition of the Follies will be held open until she has recovered from the injuries she sustained. My policy is to stand behind all my girls when they are in trouble.

And Imogene, her blonde hair tousled on the pillow, her bruised and lacerated arms lying on a silken blanket cover, held interview after interview telling reporters: "I loved him, like many other little fools."

Obviously she did, for she forgave Tinney, who immediately hotfooted it to London by fast boat in a large cabin and into an even larger contract to amuse English audiences with his particular brand of humor. Imogene followed on a slow boat, her luscious looks wasted on an elderly woman who was her third-class cabin mate and preferred reading the Bible to listening to Imogene's lurid tales of love. But life in the London fog didn't bring to the lovers the surcease they thought would be theirs away from the bright lights of Broadway. The angelic countenance she presented to Mr. Tinney shortly after her arrival soon resembled the usual red-to-blue colors it was now used to. With his usual quaint sense of humor he used it as a punching bag, Imogene said. At any rate she went around London for days looking like an angel with two black eyes.

But all this didn't discourage Imogene in her pursuit of Tinney or kill her love for him. What finally finished their "beautiful love affair" was a dinner party given by fifteen persons in honor of the comedian's London triumph. Called upon to make a toast, Tinney rose, a glass of champagne in his unsteady hand, bowed to the assembled group, and staring at his loved one shouted, "There she is! She's nothing but a Cleopatra who delights to dig pitfalls for men." The other members of the dinner party, aghast at the turn affairs had taken, left the smart supper club in Jermyn Street. Imogene, clutching together, as she clutched her satin wrap, as much pride as she could manage, looked at Tinney with both hurt and indignation and walked out of his life, firmly and finally.

Somehow she managed to gather together enough money and enough sense to take her to Berlin, where as the girl who had been punched by that great comedian Frank Tinney she got into the newsreels and was discovered by the Germans. Imogene, or "Sprudeln" as the papers translated the nickname of Bubbles, photographed magnificently! U.F.A., the German film company, featured "Sprudeln" in a melodrama called *The Iron Vault* and she began her climb to movie fame. Although the picture was received with lukewarm reviews, people did write to Hollywood that Imogene Robertson,

INTERNATIONAL NEWS PHOTOS, INC.

Imogene Wilson

which was her name at that period in her life, was even more beautiful on the screen than she had been in the Follies. Vowing "never to go back to Broadway unless they spread a red carpet on it for me," and with Tinney out of her life if not completely out of her heart, Imogene forgot, or pretended to forget, the glittering street which was linked with her unhappiness.

King Alfonso of Spain, a high-spirited monarch of great charm and gaiety, was entranced when Imogene danced with him and presented her with a gemmed brooch as an official emblem of his appreciation. Henri Letellier, called the richest man in Paris, asked her to honor him by attending a house party on his yacht. She spent a week cruising in the Mediterranean with a group of jaded members of the International Set. Then back to Madrid and another meeting with Alfonso where, as one of a party of twenty, she spent a week end at the royal palace before leaving for Paris. There her adventures started in earnest. Ben Blumenthal, a motion picture impresario, offered her the feminine lead in *Samson and Delilah,* a picture that was to be made in Berlin. Imogene's life was filled with fascinating people. On the male side, she met many men who never thought of punching bags except as a means of keeping their stomachs flat and their muscles lithe.

But when the blithe Imogene boarded the train for Berlin, fully intent on keeping her picture assignment, another man in the form of a handsome Teutonic blond sausage magnate from Frankfort became the cause of a search for the missing film actress that was headlined in most of the papers on the Continent. They met in the dining car of the train as it sped on to Berlin. By the time they had reached the demitasse and cognac phase, Imogene had accepted an invitation to be a guest at a gay house party in her new friend's castle on the Rhine. Impressed with the sausage baron's pleas she forgot all about the movie she was to make and the temptress role she had yearned for. For days the company in Berlin waited for their blonde star; and for days there was nothing but silence. They grew nervous, then agitated, and finally frantic as the rest of the cast stood about being paid for what amounted to nothing but the gossip and coffee klatsches. A search was started throughout Europe and even Tinney was brought back into her life briefly as they tried to ascertain Imogene's hideaway. One bright lad from the film company tracked the fogged-out star to the castle. Reluctantly Imogene parted from her baron and soon after left Germany with the speed — and the grace — of a gazelle, but as usual under a cloud of trouble. Only this time it was because of money, the money she wouldn't or couldn't spend on paying her tremendous bills. Perhaps she wanted to return to the United States looking as she thought a movie star should look or possibly she knew that she was leaving Europe forever — and why bother about bills? Whatever the reason, Imogene came back first class, dressed in mink and proudly and prominently displaying, among other jewels, the brooch from King Alfonso.

Her destination was Hollywood. Realizing that her name conjured up scandal although she had gotten rid of the last half of it while in Europe, she decided to discard the Imogene, too. After much debate she emerged as plain Mary Nolan, the Mary presumably after Mary Magdalene who with an even worse reputation reformed and lived to become a saint. As an alias to hide a past, it was no good at all, though. Everyone recognized her angelic face, that durable face which showed no mark of the blows that destiny and masculine fists had dealt her. With her change of name came also an apparent change in character. Her first Hollywood picture was a bit in *Topsy and Eva,* followed by a fairly large part in *Sorrell and Son.* A few more pictures added to her prestige and then came stardom with *The Shanghai Lady.* As a star Imogene's salary was equal to Frank Tinney's when the stage-struck little girl from Kentucky had stood waiting for the comedian to finish his act, hoping for a smile or a word from the person she considered the greatest of all actors.

Though the world didn't know it, Tinney, who had returned to New York, found there were no worthy offers for the man who had once been considered a top-line comedian. His wife had stopped forgiving and gotten a divorce with alimony and the house in Baldwin. Without warning his health had begun to collapse. His nimble feet could no longer dance or even support him without a cane, and his nimble tongue became so thick that he could barely speak his lines. After a long siege in hospitals and sanitariums, he emerged a wreck. The million he had earned so easily had slipped through his fingers and now that he needed it so sorely, it was gone. His wife could not collect alimony and even the house she owned went up in flames. There was only one refuge, the Philadelphia home of his father, who had tried desperately and vainly to teach his bright but irresponsible son that he ought to put some of his money away. With Frank, to act as his nurse and working for nothing, went Spaulding, his faithful Negro valet. His father and his valet were the only friends he had in adversity.

In Hollywood trouble and unhappiness were never far from Imogene's side. In 1935 she sued a producer for $500,000 on charges that he beat her (did she bring out the sadist in men?) and in 1937 she was sentenced to jail for an unpaid dress bill. Finally the scene shifts to the Actors' Fund Home in Amityville, New York, where she lived, sick and broke, for a time. Then her health came back and 1939 found her again in Hollywood, where she lived in disconsolate loneliness until she was removed to a hospital, suffering from malnutrition. Her beauty had gone, ravaged by the abuse to which she subjected it, and she was trying to be a writer — of all things. She sold her life story to a magazine and was negotiating for movie rights when, finally and kindly, death came to her at the age of forty-two in her Hollywood bungalow. After all her lovers had done to her, death must have seemed almost like a friend.

chapter seven

Perhaps the brightest and certainly one of the most memorable of all Ziegfeld's stars was Marilyn Miller. She was the twinkle-toed, dainty darling of a gaudy, poignant era that defied rationalization, caricature and prohibition. An era that Scott Fitzgerald wrote his books for; when a Stutz Bearcat went with a raccoon coat, a derby and a gold football dangling from every player's watch chain. Everyone, young and old, danced the Charleston. "Speakeasy" became as well known in the American language as atom bomb is today. And before the cellar doors of numerous brownstone houses, rich and poor alike, depending on the neighborhood, people held up membership cards as the slides in the peepholes were pushed aside. Or, more often than not, "I was here last week with Harry Brown" were the magic words that turned rusty keys or caused the grating sounds of bolts being pushed to one side to gain entrance – entrance to bars or restaurants where Scotch or a horrible facsimile thereof was served in bouillon cups and brandy in demitasses. It was a forbidden world of noise, smoke and music, ever on the lookout for the horrendous cry of "Raid!"

There were other words, too, words like "collegiate," "snappy" and "rumble seat." Girls and women shortened their skirts and shingled their hair, Paul (Pops) Whiteman was *the* orchestra leader of the time and "Avalon" and "Japanese Sandman" were the tunes most danced to in quieter moments. And a thin, dark composer named George Gershwin heard his "Rhapsody in Blue" played again and again. There were slickers – stiff yellow raincoats – topping unbuckled galoshes, which made walking a hazardous effort – but who cared as long as one was called "the cat's pajamas" or

INTERNATIONAL NEWS PHOTOS, INC.

Scene from the Follies of 1925

some such phrase that fairly reeked with admiration, if not endearment. Hip flasks, bathtub gin and home-brewed beer were all products of the jazz age, that Era of Wonderful Nonsense, as Westbrook Pegler has called it, when everybody, it seemed, had money to burn and burned it. And "Baby" Miller, as Marilyn was called affectionately by stagehands and stars alike, had touched stardom in the Follies two years before the advent of the roaring twenties.

Ziegfeld first saw Marilyn in Lee Shubert's Passing Show of 1915; saw her, wanted her, and following his usual formula, got her. But Marilyn's dancing and singing days started way, way before then; actually they began

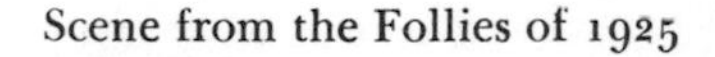
Scene from the Follies of 1925

INTERNATIONAL NEWS PHOTOS, INC.

INTERNATIONAL NEWS PHOTOS, INC.

Peacock Costumes — Follies of 1925

not long after she could walk and talk in that predetermined orbit peculiar to people who are born to be of the theatre's Milky Way. Her real name was Mary Ellen Reynolds and the combination of her own first name and her mother's, which was Lyn, started a rash of moppets with the same name that reached far beyond Findlay, Ohio, where the original was born. While she was still an infant her mother divorced her father and joined a theatrical company, the leading man of which was Oscar Miller to whom her mother was later married, and whose name Marilyn took. She made her stage debut with her mother and stepfather in August, 1903, in Lakeside, Dayton, Ohio, when she was four, as one of "The Columbian Trio." A few months later her two sisters were added to the act and it was billed as "The Five Columbians," a variety team that sang, danced and exchanged light patter.

Marilyn was known as Miss Sugarplum and she performed enchantingly, showing promise of her later ability as a dancer. Four years later the Miller family went to London, where the authorities decided that the baby and principal attraction of the troupe was too young to appear on the stage without endangering the morals of Londoners. Since they had to eat, often if not well, the act moved on to Scotland and then toured the Continent, where "Baby" Miller was permitted on stage and which meant not alone packed houses but a better chance to pay hotel bills and keep the five Millers in food and clothing. Of such necessities are artists fashioned.

Back in the United States, "Baby" and the Millers again got in a hassle with the juvenile authorities just before they were to open their act in Chicago. So the little singer and dancer had to sit quietly in the wings while in the theatre across the street Mary Miles Minter, who later became a famous movie star and was Marilyn's age, was allowed to play in *The Littlest Rebel* because she was listed as an actress. A singing and dancing child was frowned on, apparently, but an actress of whatever age was acceptable. The Millers never for a moment thought they had an actress in the family and fed up with their brushes with the law they hastily if unhappily departed for Europe once again; this time with a contract to appear in *Oh, Joy,* an English musical revue under the management of Sir Oswald Stoll.

Oh, Joy opened in Liverpool and little Marilyn was again the hit of the show, but it didn't live up to its title for the Millers. Marilyn's stepfather-manager had hot words with Sir Oswald over billing and again the troupe was "at liberty," as the ads in the theatrical papers read. After five months of scrimping and watching their savings disappear under the daily nibbles of need, they were offered a contract at London's most exclusive club — the Four Hundred — frequented by the Prince of Wales and the fashionables from Mayfair. The older Millers were received with a modicum of polite applause but it was Marilyn dressed in satin, her blonde curls topped with a silk hat and on her hands an oversized pair of white cotton gloves such as Bert Williams used to wear, who broke the British reserve. Tall and almost skinny, with her long arms and long legs moving merrily across the supper-club floor, she won her first taste of fame and her first New York engagement. The act opened in January, 1914, and by the next year Marilyn was already rehearsing for The Passing Show in which she made her Broadway debut, and Ziegfeld began plotting and planning to get her for his own.

In those days the Winter Garden, which housed The Passing Show, had a long runway leading from the stage to the rear of the orchestra seats. It was called in jest the Bridge of Thighs. This was no idle label, for the ladies of the chorus who strolled along it were bewitchingly beautiful in even more bewitching wisps of sheerest silk and a scattering of beads. It was from a seat directly under the runway that Ziegfeld first saw the blue-eyed, smiling blonde he was later to make one of the greatest of musical comedy stars. Against this loveliness of flesh and fancy the sweetness and cameo beauty of the Miller girl stood out as a string of perfectly matched pearls from Cartier might if placed alongside a carelessly tossed heap of beads on a five-and-ten counter. In her ballerina's tutu, a sparkling crown of rhinestones on her hair, her little face emerged in an exciting primness that seemed almost Victorian yet was vibrantly alive.

The last Shubert show Marilyn did was *Fancy Free,* which opened in April, 1918, and in which the reviews gave her one paragraph: "Miss Miller was always sure-fire in her dancing. She is more so now but she still misses

Marilyn Miller (right) with Fred and Adele Astaire

INTERNATIONAL NEWS PHOTOS, INC.

INTERNATIONAL NEWS PHOTOS, INC.

Marilyn Miller — 1922

much when singing or talking." Apparently it took Ziegfeld's name and sense of showmanship to bring out her talent. If Marilyn had continued with the Shuberts and done revue work only, she might never have risen to the heights of world applause she started to her climb towards in the Follies of 1918. But Ziegfeld didn't get her for his own until after many heated arguments and hot words in the Shubert offices to the effect that Marilyn was their property. They claimed that since they had weaned her along through five shows they might legitimately expect to capitalize on her now that she had found herself.

There are those who say it was Frank Carter, her first husband, who persuaded the nineteen-year-old dancer that she was ready for stardom and what better place to reach it than a show with the open-sesame label: *Florenz Ziegfeld, Jr. Production*? Carter and Marilyn met when both were at the Winter Garden. A former circus acrobat, a serious fall had caused him to abandon this line of work in favor of the stage, but he turned his acrobatic training to good account in his dancing. He was twelve years older than Marilyn, with a build a professional boxer might admire. He was full of fun and Marilyn adored him from the moment they met. But he had a serious side too. He saw to it that the dainty little dancer studied voice so that two years later in *Sally* the critics couldn't believe that the little girl with the high soprano voice they remembered so well — "Why *must* she sing?" was the way one put it — now was endearingly touching singing in a lower register. The Carters were married in 1920, went to live in the Idaho Apartments on Seventh Avenue, and for a few months were allowed to adore one another. Marilyn was happier than she had ever been or was ever to be again. She was co-starring with Leon Errol in *Sally* and she learned much from him in the way of comedy. She was the adored of the collegiate set. The boys from Princeton, Yale and Harvard made special trips to New York over week ends just to be able to stand outside the stage door and say, "Hello, Marilyn," and "Gee, your Sally is swell, Miss Miller." And at home was her husband, whom she loved passionately.

Then the first part of the honeymooon ended. Frank's show *See Saw* in which he played the juvenile lead went on the road. Sad in their first marital parting they clung to each other, trying to remember they were young and would have many more beautiful years together. Or so they thought. On Saturday night Frank called Marilyn from Pittsburgh. "Just finished my show, darling, and I'm dog-tired but I'm driving over to see my sweetheart," he said. "Wait for me!" And Marilyn with wifely concern replied: "Honey, no. I don't want you driving when you're tired. Wait until next week when the play is in Philadelphia. Please dear, you'll need the rest."

Those were the last words they ever spoke. Carter was killed instantly near Grantville, Maryland, when a new Packard he had ordered monogramed M.M. and F.C. overturned and he was pinned under the front seat.

There are those who say Carter was jealous. He was afraid Marilyn didn't want him to come to New York, worried that she'd found someone else to laugh with. But most of Broadway insisted that he was the one love of her life. And she was different, they swore, after Frank Carter died. Obviously this was the explanation for what happened later. For then the party days started. The twenty-one-year-old widow had to forget. Three hours every night she lost herself in *Sally,* but it was the hours afterwards, the hours before sleep and the blessed oblivion it brought her that had to be taken care of by laughing too much and smiling too brightly – or she might remember. No one who knew her in those days can forget her habitual entrances, whether in night clubs or at private parties. Her life was dedicated to fun. Her success was a thing to be proud of, and she was proud but always friendly to the chorus girls and extremely generous with them. You never saw Marilyn with one escort. You saw three, four or five handsome men and then you saw her. The victrola had to play constantly, the band had to shorten intermissions so that Marilyn could dance – and forget Frank Carter.

At this time Ziegfeld did for Marilyn something he had never done before for a woman star – he gave her a percentage of the receipts from *Sally.* The show ran for three years and he was notoriously openhanded with her. He'd tell her to order a new pair of shoes and she'd have thirty pairs sent over to her dressing room. Outsiders watching this got the idea that they were in love. Those who said "No" remembered she always wore the magnificent diamond necklace he had given her. Others said that Marilyn never loved anyone who was old. She couldn't. She had to live with youth. And they said Ziegfeld was still devoted to Billie Burke, and that those who really knew him felt he loved Marilyn as a father loves a daughter. That her childlike quality brought out a tender paternal feeling he didn't know he had before Patricia was born.

Forgetfulness, or a reasonable imitation, came to Marilyn two years later when the grieving Jack Pickford crossed her path. It was only natural that she and Pickford would share their mutual bereavement. They talked, he of lovely Olive Thomas and she of handsome Frank Carter, and they were drawn more and more together by their mutual bond of grief. By the time they were married in Pickfair, the fabulous Beverly Hills home of Mary Pickford and Douglas Fairbanks, Marilyn had convinced the world if not herself that she was in love. A more mature love perhaps, but then she herself had grown more mature in her young widowhood.

Ziegfeld was apprehensive and then furious for his valuable property and for her future. "Marry him and you may ruin your career," the showman warned her.

"Well, then it's good-by career," the toast of Broadway told him. "Jack is thoughtful of the little things and any woman will tell you they're what count."

That was in 1922 when there were no TV or radio microphones present but there were plenty of newsreel cameramen, reporters, photographers and celebrities on hand to witness the ceremony. Greenhouses were emptied to supply floral carpets in and around Pickfair; extra police were called to keep the curious from clambering over the garden walls; sightseeing buses reaped a harvest; and at the exact moment when Marilyn and Jack turned away from the altar as man-and-wife a plane swooped low and dropped orchids on the bridal party. "This one is for keeps," the bridal couple told everyone, "we have so much in common." They had one thing in common — temperament — and it was enough to wreck their so-called perfect union. They had quarrels and reconciliations for five years and then Marilyn decided it was futile to continue. She divorced Pickford in Paris on the prosaic grounds of desertion and neglect.

While her second marriage almost from its beginning was certain to be fated, far from the idyllic few months she had with Carter, it was not however the end of her career as Ziegfeld had predicted. In fact Marilyn had only one flop in her career and it followed after the long and exhausting run of *Sally*. She wanted to do drama. She wanted to play Peter Pan and Maude Adams had done it — why couldn't she? Ziegfeld put his foot down hard this time. But Charles Dillingham said certainly, he'd be glad to put her in *Peter Pan*, in fact he told her she *was* Peter Pan. Ziegfeld was in a rage . . . until he read the reviews which were lukewarm out of town and less than tepid when it opened in Manhattan's Knickerbocker Theatre.

Marilyn might not be the perfect Peter Pan that Barrie envisioned but she more than made up for that in her second Dillingham venture as the star of *Sunny*. It was a happy musical with the hauntingly lovely "Who?" and "D'Ye Love Me?" written by Jerome Kern, with words by Otto Harbach and Oscar Hammerstein, played by George Olsen's band. Marilyn had returned from Europe to play *Sunny* and the cast included Jack Donahue, a dancing comedian, Clifton Webb and Mary Hay, a leading comedy dance team at that time, and Cliff Edwards who sang songs as he played his ukulele and was known as Ukulele Ike. His records were musts in any record collection of the prep-school and collegiate crowd. "No Juliets for me, no grand opera either," Marilyn announced in a dressing-room interview. "Peter Pan taught me a lot. I always want to be a musical comedy actress."

In the meantime America's exponent of glorifying was getting ready for his next bit of glittering glorification by building a palatial new Ziegfeld Theatre on Sixth Avenue. He left no stone unturned to get back in his fold the little lamblike creature who had turned on him with fire of a lion when he laughed at her venture into the straight dramatic. He won, as he usually did, and Marilyn came down from Boston where *Sunny* was playing to packed houses and, dressed in a sable-trimmed broadtail coat, signed a five-year contract with Ziegfeld. "I feel much like the prodigal daughter returning home," she said, adding with a smile at the already smiling Ziegfeld, "To my mind Mr. Ziegfeld is the greatest producer in the world. His genius is positively astounding." There was much popping of photographers' lights.

His opulent production of *Rio Rita* opened the beautiful Ziegfeld Theatre on February 2, 1927, and the worlds of Broadway and Park Avenue turned out for the *première*. This had been a lifelong dream for the producer whom the papers described: "His name may start with the last letter in the alphabet but his name is first on the honor roll of the world's producers for the musical stage." It was a year of dream fulfillment for "Ziggy," as great and unknown all over America called him. Little Marilyn Miller was starring in *Rosalie* with Jack Donahue and the critics left that opening night at the New Amsterdam calling it "a regal romantic riot that must be seen by everyone." Mayor Jimmy Walker in his speech to the audience predicted a two-year run for the musical with Marilyn as the mischievous Princess of Romanza. Jack Donahue received encore after encore in the various George Gershwin and Sigmund Romberg hit tunes.

So it went, golden years for the producer and the delicately dainty star he made — twelve years all the same color, with Marilyn earning $5,000 a week — but the brush of tragedy was to paint her life again and again.

Marilyn Miller rehearsing with Jack Donahue, Gershwin, Romberg and Ziegfeld

INTERNATIONAL NEWS PHOTOS, INC.

THE ZIEGFELD CLUB

Marilyn Miller, Leon Errol and the girls in *Sally*.

In 1928 she became engaged to Ben Lyon, the Hollywood star, but that was broken off because their jobs were "too far apart"; two years later she announced she was going to marry Michael Farmer, the Irish sportsman who later married Gloria Swanson. And in 1932 it appeared in the press from a London-dated story that she would marry Don Alvarado, a movie actor. While she was in *Smiles* she was rumored engaged to Fred Astaire, with whom she was co-starred.

It was during this time that Jack Pickford, never physically strong, was taken to the American Hospital in Paris where world-famous physicians diagnosed his condition as multiple neuritis. When he knew that death was inevitable he made one last request: "I'd like to see Marilyn one more time if she isn't mad at me." She was far from angry, she was touched and eager to comply with his request. She managed to stow away after a fashion on the North German Lloyd liner *Bremen* after a midnight sailing party. Possibly as she later explained she was having such a good time that she hated to get off when the "All ashore" sounded. Or probably (and those who knew her well believed it to be so) she was trying to speed to Pickford's side before he lost his hold on life. Whichever it was she arrived in England and got no further. Before her passport difficulties could be straightened out so that she could cross the Channel and get to Paris, Pickford opened his eyes for the last time and told his nurse, "After all, I've lived more at thirty-six than most people have in a lifetime." That was his good-by in the City of Light where he had lost two of the most desirable women of the times.

There were but four years left to little Marilyn Miller, the girl whose dancing feet had carried her to fame and fortune. Four short years in which millionaire playboys and some not so boyish pursued her with offers of marriage. She made movies and she made more money and knew more success, and finally the dancing star of stage and screen (she was paid $100,000 in the screen version of *Sally*) married again. She found companionship and comfort with Chester O'Brien, chorus boy and assistant stage manager in her last starring production, *As Thousands Cheer*. They eloped one night early in October, 1934, and were married by Justice of the Peace Leo Mintzer after interrupting a barn dance in their search for a license clerk. She gave her name as Marilyn M. Pickford and said that she was twice widowed. There was no mention of divorce.

Two years later on a raw windy March day her dancing feet stopped before the window of a Fifth Avenue shop. Her deep-blue eyes widened as she looked at a dress, silken and simple, that matched her eyes perfectly. "I must have it," she said clutching her companion's arm.

"For a special occasion?" her friend inquired.

"Very special. I'm going into the hospital tomorrow — "

"And you want to wear that dress when you leave? I don't blame you. It's lovely.

"Yes. When I leave. I want to be buried in it. I am certain I won't leave the hospital alive."

Three weeks to the day, on April 7, 1936, Marilyn died at Doctors Hospital of a toxic condition following a long siege of sinus infection. Her prophetic flash of impending death was fulfilled and the twinkling toes quieted forever.

While Marilyn Miller was taking bow after bow that opening night in *Sally,* a girl with hair like a black mop of chrysanthemums, great sad eyes and a figure suggesting a John Held, Jr. drawing (the personification of the slim-hipped, flat-chested flapper) went completely unnoticed in the last row of the chorus. She couldn't have cared less, for she was a singer and it was quite by circumstances beyond her control that she was there. She had been introduced to Florenz Ziegfeld when *Sally* was in rehearsal and almost before she had realized what was going on, she was really going, too. It began when she opened her mouth prepared to sing. "Good teeth," Ziegfeld said. "Now walk over to the wall and back." Too overwhelmed to do anything but what he asked of her, she did just that. Arguing got her nowhere and a job being a job she found herself in the chorus. "I'm a singer, not a dancer," she told him when she'd managed to recapture some semblance of

Helen Morgan

PICTURE COLLECTION, NEW YORK PUBLIC LIBRARY

aplomb. But the showman was far too busy watching what was going on on the stage to bother. "You watch," she warned the girls around her, hoping her voice would carry to Ziegfeld's ears, "I'll make my mark singing or die in the attempt."

This was Helen Morgan, the girl for whom the name "blues-" or "torch-singer" was created, thus inauspiciously presented to Broadway. The thousands who were later to pay for the privilege of watching her sit on a piano and sing in a voice that James Montgomery Flagg called "a composite of all the ruined women in the world," didn't notice her that night. She was so far back that no one could see her. But singing while sitting began for Helen when she was six years old. That was when she first perched on her mother's ironing board and solemnly announced: "I will now sing Three Blind Mice." Her mother put her iron down, listened to her little daughter and told her as mothers are apt to do: "Marvelous! You will someday be a great star and make a million dollars. What will you do with it all?" Helen leaned over and kissed her and promptly said, "Spend it and give it away." She was destined, perhaps from that moment on, to do both of those things.

Helen Morgan spent part of her childhood in Danville, Illinois, where she was born, and then moved to Chicago with her widowed mother, Lulu Morgan. While still in kindergarten she first learned of tragedy and pain, the twin fates that were to follow her through most of her life. Painting Easter eggs she wiped her eyes with a pudgy little hand and smeared dye into them and was totally blind for two years. She grew up in a religious atmosphere, never missing kneeling by her bed at night and saying "Now I lay me down to sleep" long before she was sent to the Congregational Church Sunday school which was on the West Side of Chicago and a few blocks from her home. After she finished the eighth grade in public school she worked in a biscuit factory at eight dollars a week stuffing cookies and crackers into a box and sealing them up. She said at the time that it was a nice job, but she quit it because she heard of a better one — a job that paid nine dollars a week in a gelatine factory. There she took little scoops of gelatine, weighed out the proper proportions, poured the stuff in the boxes and sealed them up. "Somehow or other," she said years later, "I took a liking to the damn stuff. They caught me eating it and canned me." She found another job right away but with quite a cut in salary. She went to work in a cracker-jack factory putting prizes into the boxes — balloons, painted whistles, little American flags, children's watches and things like that — for six dollars a week. But getting into the habit of sometimes putting two in a box — "always thinking of the surprise some kid would get" — she was caught and bounced out of there.

That was her last factory job and she tried collecting delinquent bills for the telephone company, but that made her sad. Years later when asked the reason for her success her standard reply was: "Hunger."

Helen had long since given up going to Sunday school but still clung to what amounted to almost adoration of her teacher, who also taught elocution and, even more important, had a brother who was a booking agent. It was the teacher who encouraged her in her singing and talked her brother into booking the little girl with the voice that sounded as though she were swallowing sobs, into a spot in a Chicago night club. Helen's big break came while the deal was hanging fire, a break that was to take her to Broadway and make her name synonymous with the tinseled twenties. She won a beauty contest and as Miss Illinois went to Canada and was crowned Miss Mount Royal. Family friends chipped in to finance the trip and the victorious Helen later divided up the $1,500 cash prize money with them. Helen herself went on to New York City with an enterprising press agent, where she was greeted as a Canadian beauty by a burbling Mayor Hylan. Packed in her bag as carefully as the crepe-de-Chine "teddies" she was later to pack among her beaded dresses, was the stiff blue satin ribbon with the gold lettering she had worn in the contest in Canada. This was to impress theatrical agents, or so she thought in her eighteen-year-old, unworldly mind. This was before her meeting with Ziegfeld and the realization that an agent's inner office was a place she was to see only after she had hit the big time. For Helen didn't stay with the Glorifier of the American Girl very long nor did Ziegfeld urge her to. At that time Ziegfeld, by the widest stretch of the imagination, never thought that he would someday go seeking the little Morgan for one of the greatest shows he was ever to produce.

This was the time when men and women destined for stardom on Broadway and in Hollywood sang and danced in smoke-filled cellars and in attics visited by gangsters, millionaires and talent scouts. Helen became a ballad singer in Billy Rose's Backstage Club, perched on the piano and twisting a long chiffon handkerchief in and out of her slim fingers as she sang, and they called her "Camille on a piano." One version of her climb to the top of the piano was that the room was so packed she couldn't make herself either seen or heard; the other is that the late Ring Lardner, humorist-writer, lifted her on, explaining that he was always interested in helping young people up to fame. However it came about, Helen always sat on one to sing her husky blues songs, wistfully twisting the chiffon in her hands and managing to look waifishly beautiful. The late Percy Hammond, a leading drama critic of that period, called her "a raffish nightingale." The piano perch from that night on became the Morgan trademark.

While she was singing in Rose's club, George White, originator and producer of the Scandals, heard her and gave her a small singing part in his show. Helen's voice, which was perfectly pitched for a small club, wasn't big enough for a Broadway theatre; it didn't carry past the first four rows in the orchestra. White had her sit on a piano that carried a concealed microphone which in turn carried the plaintive and amplified voice as far as the theatre's foyer. As understudy to Helen Hudson, the principal of the 1925

INTERNATIONAL NEWS PHOTOS, INC.

Helen Morgan

Scandals, Helen's chance came when Miss Hudson became ill on opening night and the magical Morgan opened the show. Opened it with wild applause and an even wilder beating of her heart as she walked out on the stage scared, knowing that her big chance was here and suppose she flubbed it? But Helen didn't flub it. From that moment on her voice was what it was later called by Chicago's *Journal of Commerce* Claudia Cassidy: "A voice with the note of heartbreak — authentic heartbreak worth its weight in theatre gold."

Helen spent a thousand and one nights in the smoke-filled, dimly lighted night clubs and managed to wring the hearts of everyone who listened to her. But she remained more or less a little girl lost, carefree and gay though she seemed on the surface. Four night clubs bore her name in rapid succession; Helen Morgan's 54th Street Club, Chez Helen Morgan, Helen Morgan's Summer House and finally as some one remembered, and it was a natural, The House of Morgan. Any resemblance to it and its Wall Street namesake was coincidence on the part of a press agent. The Summer House was raided by Federal Agents in 1928 and Helen was charged with maintaining a nuisance where liquor was sold. Texas Guinan, the blonde throaty-voiced mistress of ceremonies of "Hello, Sucker!" fame, rushed to her defense. "They got the wrong party, as usual," Miss Guinan said, her voice seething with sarcasm. "She's just a dumb kid." A jury acquitted the "dumb kid" and Helen resumed the pace that was killing her.

"I feel like I'm busted inside," she told friends, but forgot about it or pretended to when Ziegfeld offered her the coveted but arduous role of Julie in *Show Boat,* his beautiful musical based on Edna Ferber's story. In making *Show Boat,* Ziegfeld set out to do something he had never done in his years of producing from the time he started out with Sandow through all the years of the Follies. He became with this venture the world's greatest producer of musical shows. The sets by Joseph Urban were amazing even for Ziegfeld; heretofore a musical play was a mere stereotype done in two acts and as many scenes, with the main setting usually in a country club, a ballroom or the lobby of a hotel. Ziegfeld saw in *Show Boat* his golden opportunity to get away from this sort of thing. He envisioned the colorful life on the levees of the Mississippi. He blended together stevedores, deck hands, troupers of the old show boats, the river men and women, the belles and beaux of the South, and all the phantasmagoria that made up life along the river in the early nineties.

And always in his two acts, the first with eight scenes and the second with eleven, there was interwoven Jerome Kern's lovely lilting music and Oscar Hammerstein's libretto. This operetta-melodrama-vaudeville-revue, as one critic termed it, leaned none too lightly on the shoulders of the cast. It was acting at its finest with Charles Winninger playing the part of Cap'n Andy and Edna May Oliver as Parthy Ann Hawks. Lovely Norma Terris

THE ZIEGFELD CLUB

Ziegfeld with members of the original *Show Boat* cast.

was Magnolia and sang "Can't Help Lovin' That Man," Jules Bledsoe's "Old Man River" brought fame to him and his "River," but it was Helen Morgan as Julie who became the star. As the troubled half-caste, the leading lady of the river boat, she sang "Bill" in her tearful voice and made the audience grieve when her fate drove her to despair, self-sacrifice and drink.

She was making real money now and spending it as fast as she could; in one year she made $117,000 but wound up $4,000 in debt. From the theatre she dashed to a night club and sang her heart out and into the hearts of the men and women who packed the club night after night. She loved people as much as they loved her and her greatest joy was to share her good fortune. One Christmas Eve she rejoined her table at a night club after tripping through a host of well-wishers on her way to the powder room. There were tears in her eyes, tears that threatened to run down and over her silver-fox cape. "That poor woman in there has to work tonight when she should be home with her family," Helen sobbed. The tears were still in her eyes when she climbed on a piano and went to work herself. Later in the powder room the elderly attendant wept as Helen thrust a hundred dollars into her hands.

There were other such gestures of her carefree and generous way. Once a chorus girl on leaving the theatre in front of Helen felt her too-thin coat jerked off her in the bitter cold night and supplanted by Helen's warm ermine; a scrubwoman on her way to work in the Harlem dawn had a wad of bills stuffed into her hand. Helen had collected money from both of her escorts and adding fifty of her own listened attentively as the old woman murmured, "May you live to be a thousand years old and have a thousand blessings." The next day her two escorts received a note and their money back because, wrote Helen, *I want these blessings all to myself and now they belong to me.*

She thought that she had found time for romance when, in 1933, she met and married Maurice Maschke, Jr. of Cleveland, but the marriage ended in a Los Angeles divorce court two years later. Helen's decree was granted on charges of cruelty yet she ruefully admitted out of court: "I'm just too busy to be a wife. It seemed like we never had a moment to ourselves." Helen had by this time finished her three years' run in *Show Boat,* had equaled her success as Addie in Hammerstein's *Sweet Adeline,* and had gone back to the Ziegfeld Follies. She went to Hollywood to play Julie and always and inevitably came back to singing on a piano in night clubs. She tried marriage again in July of 1941 when, comfortably clad in a pair of dark-blue slacks, she wed Lloyd Johnson, a Los Angeles businessman, in Miami Beach. That marriage lasted until October and it wasn't through any fault of hers that this wasn't the happily-ever-after life she dreamt about when time allowed her to dream. For on October 8, 1941, the world learned that Helen Morgan was dead. She died of a liver ailment that had been recurring since childhood, in a room in Chicago's Henrotin Hospital about the size, or so it seemed, of the speakeasies where she began the career that brought her fame. The fortune her mother had predicted many years before, she had spent and given away. "Why Was I Born?" she used to sing over and over, and the world had an answer for it. She died penniless but she did leave one fortune — a fortune in friends, and her fame as part of an era that will not be forgotten.

Flo Ziegfeld with *Show Boat* chorus

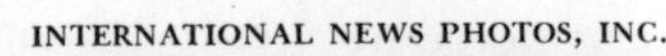
INTERNATIONAL NEWS PHOTOS, INC.

chapter eight

In all the long and spectacular years of Ziegfeld's reign, an incredible number of young women contributed their fascination — whether that of body alone or of their talents for singing, dancing, and comedy — and an astonishing number of men furnished their special talents. And what then, some have asked with a slight carping tone, did Ziegfeld give? He gave the master's touch, the true entrepreneur's sense of proportion and timing, the quality that brought all these things into form and focus; that made each Ziegfeld production, whether the Follies, a revue or an extravaganza, different from any other and an artistic entity in itself. If you want to cavil you may say that Ziegfeld had a formula, and of course you will be right — he did. But it was not a formula in the meaning of a doctor's prescription that can be refilled exactly as first prescribed. It was, rather, a changing pattern held within the basic confines of certain fundamental concepts (like a Japanese painting, for example) but within those confines fluid and moving. This applies equally to the stars and to Ziegfeld's girls, and it is of both that I would like to talk now in trying to present to you a kind of glittering kaleidoscope of the Ziegfeld era.

Even though a whole generation has grown up since the last Ziegfeld girl strutted her feathers and her figure in the spotlight, to have been a Ziegfeld girl still conjures up such adjectives as *alluring, enchanting, fascinating* and *exciting*. Their types were as varied as it was possible to find — from the full-blown lusciousness of Nita Naldi to the Madonna-like loveliness of Billie Dove, both of whom were later to become silent-picture stars. But Ziegfeld's genius also reached out, far out, in other directions — he

THEATRE COLLECTION, NEW YORK PUBLIC LIBRARY

Gladys Glad

Nita Naldi

recognized talent and knew how to develop it. His was a double-door institution. Through the stage door entered the unknowns or comparative unknowns who later gazed entranced at the front of the theatre where their names were spelled out in lights. His musicians were the best: George Gershwin, Irving Berlin, Victor Herbert, Jerome Kern, Rudolf Friml and Sigmund Romberg, to name a few. His sets were done under the mastery of Joseph Urban, the Viennese-born painter, sculptor and architect who later designed the Ziegfeld Theatre. And there were the breath-taking tableaux by Ben Ali Haggin, who reproduced famous paintings in life poses.

It was through Haggin's subtlety that Ziegfeld could become the first producer to put nude models on the stage. It was not done merely to display nudity, as Ziegfeld carefully explained time and time again with the grave demeanor of a moralist, nor was it merely an excuse for exploiting it. If a chosen masterpiece showed an undraped figure it was represented faithfully, as it was in the original. When other producers later copied him, Ziegfeld announced to the world: "These orgies of nakedness are disgusting, worse than one can find in the lowest dives in Europe and they make one ashamed of ever having anything to do with revues." But that they were both shocking and delighting to a slightly jaded Broadway, Ziegfeld hadn't any doubts. He had only to listen to the names called out to chauffeurs by the stage doorman nightly — such Social Register names as Guggenheim, Rhinelander Stewart, Vanderbilt, Biddle, Hutton — to know that his daring and artistry were paying off.

As I have pointed out, these were naïve days along the Great White Way and both Ziegfeld and Ben Ali Haggin had to ask for volunteers to stage the first of the Tableaux in which a girl was overdressed if she wore as much as a string of pearls around her throat. Kay Laurell was the original volunteer to offer her services, and after her debut as "September Morn" she posed sitting undraped atop a huge globe with soft lights playing over it. Another time she stood at the mouth of a cannon, only slightly draped with the French flag and a fluttering flag at that. It was the story along Broadway in those days that Ziegfeld had to have two cannoneers standing

Kay Laurell

THEATRE COLLECTION, NEW YORK PUBLIC LIBRARY

Kay Laurell

THEATRE COLLECTION, NEW YORK PUBLIC LIBRARY

near Kay to keep her from dropping it. Her name became a synonym for undraped feminine loveliness and Kay was more than willing to have it remain as such. She knew she had a beautiful figure, slender like a boy's but softly rounded, and that it was her greatest asset on the road to fame. Ned Wayburn, who staged so many of the Follies, called Kay "the original American Venus."

But Kay was more than that, she was shrewd, ambitious, self-centered and lived in a world of calculating dreams. She would do anything to call attention to herself, figuring that she could build up her fame as a serious actress and satisfy a yearning that the former telephone operator from Erie, Pennsylvania, had had long before she ever put on her headphones and started pushing plugs into a switchboard. She would happily have ridden around Times Square as Lady Godiva if her press agents had asked her. She knew she was lovely and saw no reason for concealing it. Her life was planned in her own mind as carefully as a battle map and it was to lead to the legitimate stage and society, both spelled with a capital S. There is a story that once when she was lunching at the Plaza she jerked a glass of water from the table and then stood up, berating the waiter for his clumsiness. The effect of the scene as Kay stood up, all eyes turned on her, was exactly the desired one. She attracted attention to herself and there were murmurs through the dining room of: "Who is that beautiful woman?"

She let other Follies girls keep late hours and go on champagne parties. That was all right for the "dubs," she used to say while her restless ambition kept nipping at her heels. She studied French, she studied dancing and music. She took lessons in deportment, in poise and speaking. She took up golf, tennis and riding — anything to help along her wistful desire to acquire a finishing-school manner, to get her into international society and make her able to meet anyone in the world with ease. Soon after the first World War Kay left the Follies. She went to Hollywood for a while but her chiseled type of beauty didn't screen well. Back in New York she went through months of grueling apprenticeship in stock. She played for a while with the Broadway Players in Yonkers and spent ten months with A. H. Woods' farce *Ladies' Night.* Later she had a leading role in *Whispering Wires,* which ran for many months on Broadway. She studied under one of the leading actors of the Comédie Française and played in French with an American company in Paris headed by Clark Silvernail, of which Peggy Wood was a member. But as an actress she never received real acclaim. Ironically, her fame lay behind her in the Follies, which she had given up. Her real life was a dream and like most dreams it never came true.

Certainly the life of a Follies girl wasn't all champagne and caviar. It couldn't be, for no life is, especially one built around a career. There were arduous hours of rehearsals, costume fittings and cues to learn always under the zealous Ziegfeld. That the girls worked hard I don't doubt but that they worked long hours with rehearsals sometimes lasting until dawn or as rumor had it, until the girls fainted from exhaustion, is hard to swallow, as is the story that the girls would not allow their private lives to interfere with their work in the theatre. There is a legend that they all married millionaires – many of them did, so many that Will Rogers once quipped: "We have a hard time keeping our girls together, especially on tour. Everytime we get to a new town some of them marry millionaires, but in a few weeks they catch up with the show again."

Of the dozen more or less who married into European nobility a dark-haired little dancing girl, slender and lovely, captured both a title and a millionaire when she married Lord Charles Cavendish, second son of the Duke of Devonshire and a member of one of the most affluent and aristocratic families in England. Her name was Adele Astaire. She left Broadway for Lismore Castle, the Irish country seat of the Devonshires, and she left behind her brother Fred, with whom she danced, and a world of admirers who were to miss her but who wished her well.

In the true sense of the word Adele was not a Ziegfeld girl; she didn't parade in beads and baubles nor was she known for her beauty. (She was a five-foot girl with a warm smile and hoydenish enchantment.) Fred and Adele Astaire, as they were billed with Marilyn Miller in *Smiles,* were the outstanding brother-and-sister twosome in the world when Ziegfeld starred them in his own theatre in the show which opened on November 18, 1930. Dancing seemed to be a natural gift to both of them. They received their dancing lessons in Omaha, Nebraska, where their father was a brewer, and prohibition turned them into professionals when the brewery succumbed to Volstead. Through the Mid-West their salaries kept mounting with their bookings. Broadway, as Broadway invariably does, soon heard of their enormous success and they made their debut with Ed Wynn and Justine Johnstone in *Over the Top* in 1917. Subsequently they appeared in The Passing Show of 1918, *Apple Blossoms, The Love Letter* (with John Charles Thomas) , *Stop Flirting,* which marked their first London triumph in 1923, *Lady Be Good,* and *Funny Face.* Adele's flair for comedy was first evinced in *Love Letter,* and with the years she developed into a popular comedienne.

It was while Adele was appearing in the Ziegfeld hit that rumors of her engagement to such men about town as John Hay Whitney, William B. Leeds, Jr. the wealthy British woolen merchant, William Gaunt, Jr., and so many others that as one wit remarked: "Had she married them all Peggy Hopkins Joyce would be a piker." It was while the fleet-footed team was starring in *The Band Wagon* that Adele announced her engagement to Lord Charles and her retirement from the world of New York, Paris and London, where the brother-and-sister singing and dancing act had become the rage. "It's an honest-to-goodness retirement," she said.

INTERNATIONAL NEWS PHOTOS, INC.

Fred and Adele Astaire arriving in New York on the S.S. *Majestic*

"There will be no succession of last appearances, either. Fred is quite competent to continue his career without me." Adele plunged confidently into the life of a British noblewoman and Fred, perhaps with not quite as much confidence, went into the movies. He revolutionized the filming of screen musicals and worked out his own dance routines. His partners have included Ginger Rogers, Joan Crawford, Joan Fontaine, Rita Hayworth, Leslie Caron and Audrey Hepburn. He has the knack of making his dancing look like fun and today is one of the film world's celebrities who is also mentioned in *Who's Who in America.* He was married for many years to Phyllis Livingston Potter, daughter of Dr. Harold Baker of Boston, and when she died in 1954, she left Fred with three children, Peter Potter, her son by a former marriage, Fred, Jr., and a daughter Ava.

Adele true to her word, never returned to the stage. She might have, had World War II not turned the world into a holocaust. Shortly before, her husband, the gay successful young Lord Charles, died suddenly in their ivy-covered castle in Ireland. When war came it gave her a chance to work out her grief. She became a member of the famous Rainbow Corner in London where thousands of servicemen found a touch of their homeland while in England. With the war's end Adele returned home and met Kingman Douglass, member of an old Chicago family, and for the second time in her life really fell in love. They were married on April 28, 1947 in Warrenton, Virginia. Today she leads the quiet life of a country squire's wife at Middleburg. She entertains graciously, keeps in touch with friends, and her interests are horses, dogs, gardening — and her way of living.

"America's loveliest woman" was the title bestowed on Justine Johnstone by such noted artists as Henry Hutt, Harrison Fisher and Penrhyn Stanlaws. Ziegfeld dubbed her his American beauty and the theatre world called her the most beautiful blonde on Broadway. She was all this and also the most photographed girl in New York in 1915 when Irving Berlin's first musical, *Watch Your Step,* starring Vernon and Irene Castle, was enchanting thousands. In the cast-listing Justine's name was in tiny type but her blonde radiance did not go unnoticed and, despite the rave reviews of the stars' performances, one critic found time and space to write: "Justine Johnstone looked very pretty in the first act." But she was more than pretty with her wealth of natural blonde hair, her blue eyes and a skin that was pink and white and protected at all times from the sun, a symbol of femininity in those pre-tanning days. Justine, her figure reedlike and slim with the rounded curves of a young girl, was indeed the epitome of American womanhood. *Girlhood* would perhaps be a better word, for Justine had been out of high school only a brief two years when she crossed by ferry from her home in Hoboken to conquer Broadway. The Theatre was to be her life and Maude Adams was her idol.

Before Justine placed her dainty feet on what she considered the right side of the footlights her beauty lead her to become one of New York's youngest and most famous photographers' models. When the First International Exposition of Photographic Arts opened at the Grand Central Palace such judges as Minnie Maddern Fiske and Alfred Stieglitz chose Justine's picture as winner in the "Beauty Contest" with a prize of $5,000. Ziegfeld found her — it was a natural that he would — and added her to the already legendary list of his famous blondes: Marion Davies, Dolores, Lillian Lorraine and Ina Claire were Follies girls at the time, swirling velvets and chiffons across the stage with headdresses so elaborate that their fair young heads could hardly hold them up, or so it seemed. In the World War I years there was generally a patriotic theme running through the Follies and thus, in 1916, the curtain was brought down on a tableau that revealed Justine as Columbia wrapped in the American flag. Kay Laurell was the Dove of Peace and Bert Williams sang a song called "I'm Neutral."

While her beauty was a delight to audiences (and secretly it must have been to her), Justine also found that it was a handicap for someone who yearned for the legitimate stage. She was just too beautiful, it seemed to other producers and certainly to Ziegfeld, to bother with the training and techniques that go into the making of a serious actress. After she left the Follies, Justine was starred in the musical, *Over the Top*. Somewhere around the same time Justine Johnstone's Little Club opened, where the gay young people around town paid a fifty-dollar membership fee and flocked in droves to make champagne flow. She was the reigning beauty in the cast of *Oh Boy* at the Princess Theatre, but nobody seemed to care if she could sing or dance or had the making of another Ethel Barrymore; it was enough just to be able to look at this ethereal creature. But it wasn't enough for Justine.

The theatre world was shocked and puzzled when she deserted Broadway to join a stock company in Waterbury, Connecticut. She said quite simply that she wanted to be an actress and that therefore she had to learn to act and that she couldn't do it in the Follies or musical comedies. To a baffled Broadway this was insane. She had her name in lights, the stage-door Johnnies lined up every night with jewels and orchids, and she was as well known as anyone could hope to be. What more could she want?

Justine knew what she wanted and what people said didn't matter. She studied, watched and learned during her time in Waterbury with a deter-

Gertrude Vanderbilt

THEATRE COLLECTION, NEW YORK PUBLIC LIBRARY

Ina Claire

INTERNATIONAL NEWS PHOTOS, INC.

mination that was almost dedication. She drove around the town in her blue National roadster, usually accompanied by a tall handsome man who seemed to share all her non-working hours. He was Walter Wanger, the Hollywood producer, and no one in the little Connecticut city was a bit surprised when she married him.

Following their marriage the Wangers went to London where he directed at Covent Garden, and the young Mrs. Wanger worked at being both an actress and manager. There followed a few brilliant years when Justine made perhaps not the mark of success she had once dreamed about that day on the Hoboken ferry, but satisfying success in the movies and on the stage as a comedienne. But the theatre world began to pall and about this time, with no medical or scientific background or training, she felt drawn to pathological research. It might have been the comfort of a world where her outward beauty would not be given priority over her inward intelligence. Whatever it was, Justine joyfully laid aside her furs and jewels for the pristine white-starched coat of a pathologist. It was in New York, at the College of Physicians and Surgeons, that she entered the laboratory as a serious worker and started to learn her new profession from the beginning. Doctors who worked with her during those student years talk often of the quickness of her perception and her retentive memory. By 1931, though she had no medical degrees, she reached the distinction of being an acknowledged collaborator of Dr. Harold Hyman Thomas and Dr. Samuel Hirschfield, and as Justine Wanger she was not identified as a former Follies beauty. On April 14, 1940, Broadway rubbed its eyes when the papers announced that one of its fairest had been one of the scientific minds behind the sensational five-day cure for syphilis. Her friends and colleagues said that from the beginning of her scientific life, during and between experiments, she had been specializing in the causes of cancer and other dread diseases.

Her divorce in 1938 ended what Hollywood considered a marriage of devotion. Wanger has since married Joan Bennett. Justine, in California now and living for her research, described her switch from the footlights to the lights over a microscope as "the story of a person who made a shift in her interests." It is more than that; it is the story of a beautiful woman, and the proof that beauty and brains are more compatible than anyone ever suspected back in the days of the Ziegfeld Follies.

It was almost a certainty that many of the glorified girls of the Follies would eventually become the glamour girls of Hollywood. It didn't matter if they could act in the early days of motion pictures; and who cared if an ethereal-looking girl spoke with a Yankee twang or a rosebud mouth uttered pure Brooklynese? Beauty was Hollywood's best buy in the days of the silent silver screen. So it was only natural that where beauty was to be found in abundance, so too in abundance were the movie scouts with their contracts ready to be signed on the dotted line. Ziegfeld was first flattered, then chagrined, and finally fearful that this new type of amusement might eventually hurt the theatre and especially him. When motion pictures became dangerously popular he started a campaign against them in paid advertisements which read: ZIEGFELD FOLLIES — *Glorifying the American Girl in the flesh . . . not canned.* Although movies and radio became deadly enemies (so he thought) he relented once for the sake of a stage novelty — and he was always on the search for something different and eye-appealing — and used a movie screen in one of his Follies. Mae Murray was seen rushing down a street from afar in a movie and popped through the screen in person just as she reached the near end. It was amusing to the audience and certainly a novelty in those days but Ziegfeld would have no more of the films. But his girls did and many of them became, and still are, stars of both silent and talking films.

Paulette Goddard with her chestnut hair and unabashed grace was a pert, pretty, stage-struck high school girl when her uncle, Charles Goddard, introduced her to Ziegfeld. Paulette was attending high school in Great Neck, Long Island, and biology and Latin were beginning to pall when she remembered Uncle Charlie was a friend of the famed producer. Hadn't she heard him speak of Flo often, if not intimately? Uncle Charlie agreed to sponsor her and when she was hired she changed her name from Marian Goddard Levee to the unusual Paulette and used her middle name in honor of Uncle Charlie. She was a show girl in Ziegfeld's *Rio Rita* and her role was short but enough to call attention to her lovely legs, beguiling shoulders and her young body. She was known as "the girl on the moon." It was a cardboard moon and Paulette did nothing but smile (and this was genuine) at the audience which in return smiled back. It was her first taste of success and triumph and was later to lead her to millions and marriages.

Years later she said in an interview that show girls were far more frivolous in the days of the Ziegfeld extravaganzas because of the lavish productions and the fact that nothing more was expected of them than to parade before the footlights in that wonderfully exaggerated, alluring way. "I could tap," she said, "but I was never given the chance. Ziegfeld used to say I was a great sitter. I sat, and I walked. I didn't mind. I was young and I was able to pay for my own lessons at Ned Wayburn's. Mother was earning $25 a week in a dress shop and life seemed to hold everything I wanted at the time." Ziegfeld, in a burst of generosity, once sent Paulette and Susan Fleming (later married to Harpo Marx) to Palm Beach. "We were his pets," she recalled. "He guessed we'd each catch ourselves a millionaire. In two weeks I was engaged to one but when I told him I was only fifteen, he dropped me cold." Paulette's biography gives her date of birth as June 3, 1911. But like her marriage to Chaplin and so much of her life, this is shrouded in mystery. On a Hollywood questionnaire, when asked when she was born she wrote: "Oscar Wilde and Goddard say 'Any woman who tells her age tells anything.' "

After her Palm Beach days Paulette became filled with ambition and with a passion for money and exotic cars. "Very Peg O'My Heart" (a play about a waif who became a duchess) was the way she put it. She wore short black gloves, short satin dress and was seldom seen without a small dog carried carefully in her arms. These appointments belonged to the sophisticates, so she thought. World-weary though she tried to seem, she nevertheless married Edward James, president of the Southern States Lumber Company, and gave up the tall buildings of New York for the pine trees of Asheville, North Carolina. She played hostess, learned to hunt, wanted to work,

Paulette Goddard

INTERNATIONAL NEWS PHOTOS, INC.

Susan Fleming

INTERNATIONAL NEWS PHOTOS, INC.

but Mr. James' answer was always a firm "No" — and nearly died of boredom. Paulette always spoke of him as a generous, warm friend but finally to his no-work slogan she added her own no-marriage, and that was the end of that. However, generous friend he must have been, for she drove to Hollywood by way of Reno in a Duesenberg.

While she was dancing one night at the Cocoanut Grove, a man stopped her and asked if she would come to his office the next morning for a screen test. Hesitating until she asked if she could bring her mother (who was far, far from Hollywood at that time) she went, passed the test with flying colors, and landed a job with the Hal Roach Studios at $100 a week. It lasted six months. After that she did a show-girl bit in *The Kid From Spain* starring Eddie Cantor. She was far from being nominated the girl Hollywood couldn't do without, but her life was filled socially with extravagant cars, yachting parties, and just plain parties (if you could call any party in those early Hollywood days plain). And about this time she met Charlie Chaplin, who signed her to an exclusive contract. "Charlie understood me," was the way she put it later in a reminiscent mood. "You know, most people look better with their shoes on but I don't. Without shoes, well, call it an animal quality that some people have found useful — the gamin type, the barefoot actress."

Whatever it was, Chaplin cast her, after a lengthy and well-publicized search for "not necessarily an actress but a beautiful girl," in *Modern Times*. The picture took two years to make and throughout that time Paulette's photographs were given world-wide attention. With her mother she went on a world tour with Chaplin on his yacht. When they reached Canton, China, the young actress and her comedian mentor were married. No members of the press were on hand and no one in far-off Hollywood heard about it. The wedding took place in 1936 and when they returned to the cinema city rumors of their marriage were hinted in the various columns. They asked was Paulette not only his protegée but also his bride? But the marriage remained unconfirmed until she obtained a divorce from the comedian in Juarez, Mexico, six years later. By that time Paulette was one of Hollywood's biggest stars. With her brilliant success, her shrewd business sense which enabled her to make unusually advantageous contracts for herself, and with her popularity and personality, she enjoyed life to the full. "I have fun just living," she would say.

As her movie career made her one of the wealthiest women in Hollywood (she was winning additional repute as one of the best dressed), Paulette found more time to travel and more time for the fun she loved. In New York she celebrated her thirty-first birthday (so she said) at a party attended by Mrs. W. K. Vanderbilt, Woolworth Donohue, Winston Guest and other New York socialites. After her marriage to Burgess Meredith in the garden of the Beverly Hills home of film producer David O. Selznick, she and her actor husband journeyed to Dublin to present *Winterset*. Paulette played the leading feminine role in the drama, and Dublin critics were enthusiastic over her performance. But their marriage was hopeless from the start: Paulette with her keen love of life, quick mind and bright beauty was nevertheless utterly realistic and rated money as the most important thing in the world, whereas Meredith was artistic, vague and haphazard. They tried to make a go of it but the roads they wished to travel were too diverse. They were divorced in Cuernavaca, Mexico, five years later. Today Ziegfeld's moon girl lives mostly in Paris, London, St. Moritz and Rome. There are rumors of her marriage to author Erich Remarque and the aura of mystery that has always surrounded her is still there. Somewhere above the fleecy white cloud of gaiety and laughter Paulette's moon still rides the skies.

Irene Dunne, so often described as Hollywood's loveliest lady,with the accent on the latter, started her career with ambitions of becoming a Shakespearean actress. She visualized herself as Portia, Desdemona, and especially as Juliet in the balcony scene. When only five years old, in a yellow tarlatan dress, she earned her first pay check cavorting about the green in an outdoor performance of *A Midsummer Night's Dream* in Madison, Indiana. A rather unusual beginning for a girl who was later to come under Ziegfeld's magic, and magic it was for her, too. But then Irene's career, from the beginning when she left home to teach kindergarten in Chicago until her meeting with Ziegfeld and eventual Hollywood stardom, was different, to say the least, from that of others who came under the master showman's touch. Different, and yet, as so often, it followed the pattern from Ziegfeld to zenith.

Irene went to Chicago to teach, but as her application from the Board of Education hadn't come through she decided to try out for a scholarship in the elder Ziegfeld's Chicago College of Music. She had been taking singing lessons twice a week at home, spending her allowance on Tetrazzini recordings, and at high school commencement night she had sung an aria from *Louise* that had received far more than polite applause. She won the scholarship and spent "two divine years with nothing but music in my life," graduating with a medal for vocal proficiency. Then, like most young singers, she packed and prepared to come to New York. The senior Ziegfeld had a practical career in mind for her: "You must go see my son Florenz," he told her. To Irene, Florenz could wait; the Metropolitan Opera couldn't — or so she dreamed. But arriving in New York she learned "they could wait and did. I was too young, too skinny, too inexperienced, too everything."

Irene again applied to the Board of Education for her teaching license and while waiting made the rounds of auditions and managers' offices with a friend of her mother's who was launching a daughter of her own on a singing career. One morning at the Roxy Theatre when the road company of *Irene* was being cast, a little man in a black hat shouted at her, "What

INTERNATIONAL NEWS PHOTOS, INC.

Irene Dunne

are you here for? Do ya sing?" Irene was on the verge of remarking haughtily that she sang nothing but classical music when he said, "C'mon kid, let's hear ya." She stood up and sang "Kiss Me Again," very badly as she remembers but it more than satisfied the little man for she was given the singing lead. Two months of the color, change and excitement of being on the road, and the fever of the theatre began to shut out her determination for opera. Then, back to Broadway and parts in *Clinging Vine, City Chap* and *Sweetheart Time,* and a meeting with Ziegfeld.

"I was going up in an elevator to keep an appointment at the New Amsterdam Theatre," she said in an interview when she first arrived in Hollywood, recalling fondly that she had spent ten dollars on a large straw hat with a chiffon lining and wore a dress in her favorite color, blue. "A number of other girls were in that elevator and so was Mr. Ziegfeld. When we reached the ninth floor, all of the girls except myself got off and Mr. Ziegfeld followed them. My appointment was on another floor.

"A little while later, even though I was in another theatrical office, Mr.

Ziegfeld's secretary walked in and said that Mr. Ziegfeld had sent her to find out the name of the girl in the large hat and blue dress. 'Irene Dunne,' I answered, somewhat startled.

" 'Well, Mr. Ziegfeld wants to talk with you.'

" 'I'm sorry,' I stammered, 'but I won't be able to see him. I've just agreed to take a part in another show and I'm here to sign my contract.' "

She never saw him again until he was casting the Chicago company of *Show Boat,* when, after trying out several Magnolias, he suddenly remembered the girl in the elevator and sent for her. By this time her teaching application had arrived and with it an offer of a class at Public School 141, but Irene sent it back with a polite thank-you, having signed with Ziegfeld and decided that she didn't want to be a teacher after all.

"That was the end of another dream too," she said, "the dream of playing Juliet. The nearest I ever got to the balcony was in *Show Boat* when, in my role of Magnolia Hawks, I first met the dashing gentleman-gambler Ravenal. Leaning over the top deck of Cap'n Andy's old theatrical barge, 'Cotton Blossom' Magnolia throws a rose to her handsome River Romeo on the docks below. Then, instead of the classic lines of The Bard of Avon, Allan Jones and I burst into a Jerome Kern song. Allan and I put our lungs into it with as much earnestness as if we really had been doing a Shakespearean play."

On the opening night at the Illinois Theatre she recognized Ziegfeld sitting in the audience, in the second row. Though only separated from him by that short distance, he sent her a telegram backstage at the end of the first act. It read:

WITH YOU IN THE CAST AS MAGNOLIA I KNOW THAT MY CHICAGO COMPANY IS SAFE NOW. CONGRATULATIONS. ZIEGFELD.

It was during the run of *Show Boat* that a film scout from RKO studios asked Irene to luncheon. All she remembers is that he ate kippered herring, talked constantly and kept shoving a contract, along with a leaky pen, under her nose. She signed over the dessert because "I wanted to see the movie stars out there." Arriving in Hollywood, 3,000 miles from the Metropolitan (which she still hoped to conquer some day), she walked up and down the Hollywood hills every day doing scales against the time when she would return to New York — and opera. Her first film part was in *Present Arms,* and after seeing it Irene remarked, "I might just as well have continued walking up and down the hills." Then came another picture, *Leathernecking,* and more hills and more scales until finally the chance to play opposite Richard Dix in the 1931 Academy Award's *Cimarron,* and with it stardom. This was a film version of Edna Ferber's book and Irene played her part so magnificently that when Will Rogers saw the movie he said, "The only woman I would vote to be a Congresswoman would be Irene Dunne."

Miss Dunne's career is an illuminating example of how an intelligent, integrated person can achieve the satisfaction of high artistic accomplishment despite the fact that the original goals (in her case grand opera and the Shakespearean stage) were never reached. She suffered no neurotic frustration. In fact, you cannot call her achievements a compromise, except to the extent that all of us have to compromise with life.

Ziegfeld had good reason to fear the menace of the movies. It must have been galling to him, for he was a man without much of a saving sense of humor, to be forced slowly into the recognition that his Follies were becoming a charm school for Hollywood. He would never, of course, have acknowledged this openly, to do so would have been offensive to his egotism and insufferable to his pride, yet in the aloneness of his office or in the slumberous security of his bed, he must have known it was so. The record of his girls who traveled one-way from the Follies to the big studios out West was infuriating evidence. They included, besides those already named, Billie Dove, Dorothy Mackaill, Jacqueline Logan, Lilyan Tashman, Marion Davies, Mae Murray, and others who did not climb so high a peak of prominence. The careers of some of these girls have an interest beyond that of passing mention.

Billie Dove was one of the crowned queens of the silent movie days in the days of Richard Barthelmess, Douglas Fairbanks, Sr., Milton Sills, Rod La Rocque and other mute movie heroes of that era. Her movie career literally started while she was in the Follies. To add to her income and perhaps to become known as an actress as well as a beauty, she worked as an extra at the Fort Lee studios across the river in New Jersey. Billie was born beautiful and her beauty blossomed with the years, so that by the time she was fourteen she won fame as an artist's model. She was born Lillian Bohny on May 14, 1903, in New York City, and as a child used to pose for magazine covers. So perfect were her features that artists, and later Hollywood cameramen, used to say that it was impossible to catch her at a bad angle. Ziegfeld noticed her face first on a magazine cover and promptly sent for her, but she was too young to join the Follies then. Billie remembered, and so did Ziegfeld, and when she turned sixteen he put her in the Follies as one of the favorite wives in a harem scene along with Jessica Reed, Alta King, Ruth Taylor and Margaret Irving.

But it was while she sat on a hoop, the spotlight on her slender graceful body, brown hair and enormous hazel eyes, that she attracted the attention of the movie moguls. And so this girl with a beauty as exquisitely delicate as an etching and as gentle as a dove's, or so the artists who named her called it, left Ziegfeld in a few years to become a leading lady, then a star. Ironically, although she was chosen for her beauty, her first movie role required her to wear a mask in a small part in a film which starred Conway Tearle and Elaine Hammerstein. It took her four years to reach the success of stardom;

four years of hard work and steady advancement until she leaped into prominence with *The Marriage Clause,* produced by Lois Weber, followed by a role as Douglas Fairbanks' leading lady in *The Black Pirate.* Then came a contract with First National and her name, like her beauty, became what one studio press agent called "a household word."

Although they were lovely (Ziegfeld wouldn't have a girl who wasn't or at least gave the illusion of loveliness), Gertrude Vanderbilt and Lilyan Tashman were what we would call today streamlined, svelte sophisticates. Gertrude went on from the Follies to musical comedy stardom and a romance with William J. Fallon, "the Great Mouthpiece" of the New York bar and one of the most colorful and resourceful lawyers of the times. It was of him Will Rogers once remarked as he coiled his rope and chewed his gum: "If the Germans had Bill Fallon for their lawyer, they'd have the Allies apologizing to them!" Gertrude lives quietly in New York today.

Lilyan Tashman died in 1934, died when she was still happily married to her actor-husband Edmund Lowe, and was known as the best-dressed

INTERNATIONAL NEWS PHOTOS, INC.

Billie Dove

INTERNATIONAL NEWS PHOTOS, INC.

Margaret Irving

movie star in the film colony. She died at the height of her career, suddenly and shockingly to the thousands who loved her, after an emergency operation for an advanced tumorous condition. Such was her popularity that at her funeral in New York police were called to hold back a crowd of 5,000 people, and Eddie Cantor, who had been asked to deliver the eulogy and was forced to fight his way through the crowd into the funeral chapel, remarked: "This is the most disgraceful exhibition I've ever witnessed."

But Lilyan's story began 35 years before that day, it began almost with her earliest recollections of wanting to be an actress. Her blonde hair and unusual good looks led a number of artists to use her as a model. Several attempts to get on the stage had proved fruitless and so, although she was only seventeen, she had almost given up hope when she met Ziegfeld. This was quite by chance and equally by chance was the fact that she was sitting in the old Café de Paris — this was before prohibition — when Ziegfeld entered. Possibly she hadn't recognized him when he came in and sat at a nearby table (although this is unlikely for his pictures like his girls were seen everywhere), or maybe she was too busy talking with her companion to have noticed him but, whatever it was, Ziegfeld looked at the young, stunning blonde. Shortly afterwards a strange man came up to Lilyan and announced, "Mr. Ziegfeld would like to see you." Lilyan used to say later, "I thought it was a gag. So I said, 'If Mr. Ziegfeld wants to see me tell him to come to my table.' " And Ziegfeld did just that.

He offered her a place in the Follies. Lilyan accepted with an outward mannner of nonchalance and was weeks catching her breath. Ina Claire was the star of the first show Lilyan was in, Marion Davies was in the cast and so were Marilyn Miller, Eddie Cantor, Bert Williams and Billie Dove. It was a lucky show for all of them, for they all went on to greater fame. Lilyan didn't do much — she wasn't expected to do anything but carry her costumes and headdresses with an air of languid loveliness. She was the "Symbol of Change of Emotion" in one scene and a Goldenrod in the "Garden of Girls" in another. She was in many more "episodes," as the Follies programs attest, before a desire for the dramatic stage led to a part three years later in Avery Hopwood's *The Gold Diggers* and the termination of her Follies days. This was followed by a part in *The Garden of Weeds* and a meeting with "the man who has influenced my entire life — my husband, Edmund Lowe." Belasco had taken her away from Ziegfeld and now it seemed that Hollywood was trying to take her away from Lowe, whom she had married on September 1, 1925. While playing in *Weeds* her name was up in lights but her husband out in Hollywood was too far away to see them, so she said, "It seems that although I was going to amount to something I was lonely for Eddie. Rather than be separated from him I threw away what appeared to be a promising career and followed him to Hollywood."

James Cruze gave her her first start in Hollywood, a start that led to screen portrayals symbolizing completely the era of glitter and bedazzlement. When the popularity of "smart society films" began to wane — as it did during the Depression — Lilyan survived as a unique and independent personality. Not only on the West Coast but in New York and Europe she was known for her poise, personality and clothes. No one disputed her title of being "The Best-Dressed Woman in Hollywood." Yet, she used to say, "It's more boring to hear a woman talk about clothes than to listen to a man discuss his golf score." Her stage training and her low husky voice gained her considerable popularity when Hollywood was having difficulty finding actors with proper voices for the talking pictures. Usually she played the part of a worldly-wise woman, but in *Wine, Woman and Song* she assumed the role of a self-sacrificing mother. She died the morning the reviews came out.

Honey-haired, wide-eyed Ruth Etting was catapulted to nation-wide success as a singer in a leading role in the Ziegfeld Follies of 1927. In those post-World War I days Tin Pan Alley was turning out hit after hit and Ruth was fast becoming the song girl of the Alley. The money was rolling in. Besides her income from cafés, radio and recordings she was getting $200 a week for stage appearances in movie houses. Irving Berlin had written "Remember" and Ruth was being remembered for her singing of that tantalizing tune. There were others almost as famous. Songs such as "Looking at the World Through Rose-Colored Glasses" by Gus Kahn and Walter Donaldson, "Thinking of You" and "Ramona." Ruth sang at the College Inn in Chicago's Hotel Sherman and the collegiate crowd crammed in to hear her. In fraternity houses and college dormitories Ruth, through her recordings and her soothing caress of a voice, was the sophomores' delight. But it was Ziegfeld who made her a favorite with their mothers and fathers.

She had never taken a singing lesson in her life but song writers begged to have her introduce their songs. Irving Berlin heard one of her recordings and had Ziegfeld send for her.

"He is the one who is responsible for my being in Ziegfeld shows," she said in interview after interview. "Like everyone else in show business, it was my ambition to work for Ziggie.

"I wasn't nervous that opening night of the Follies — I never was while performing — but I was thrilled. To be under a Ziegfeld-produced show was to have reached the top."

Immediately after the Follies closed in 1928, Ruth was signed for a part in *Whoopee,* starring Eddie Cantor. The next year she starred in *Simple Simon* with Ed Wynn and introduced "Ten Cents A Dance." It was a song — a story really — about a dance-hall hostess, a dime-a-dance girl; a sad, haunting tune and the first-night audience clamored for encore after encore. They applauded similarly Ruth's revival of the old Nora Bayes hit "Shine On Harvest Moon" which she introduced with tremendous popular-

INTERNATIONAL NEWS PHOTOS, INC.

Ruth Etting

ALFRED CHENEY JOHNSTON — THE ZIEGFELD CLUB

Ruth Etting

ity in the Follies of 1931, the last of the famous Ziegfeld extravaganzas. In the same Follies were Helen Morgan, Harry Richman and Jack Pearl, but it was Ruth and her old-time song, sung with what Ziegfeld once called her "me-to-you" voice, that stopped the show.

Her success, however, was a melancholy mockery — or rather, the life she was leading away from the lights of Broadway made it so. Certainly her cup of happiness brimmed to the full with adulation, but it held the poison of an aching loneliness. That loneliness was personified in "Love Me or Leave Me," another song that when sung today reminds people of "America's Sweetheart of Song" in the reckless and bountiful twenties and the dismal, despairing thirties. To understand it, one must go back into Ruth's girlhood and to her meeting with Chicago's cigar-smoking character "The Gimp," who due to an injured leg and peculiar way of walking was never called anything else. His real name was Moe Snyder.

Ruth was born on November 2, 1896, in David City, a drab little town that lay in the middle of Nebraska's fields of wheat. She was an only child and her mother died when the family made a trip to Southern California when Ruth was five years old. Her father's business required that he travel frequently and Ruth stayed with an aunt and grandmother for the next eleven years, going through the process of growing up in a small town. She attended prayer meetings in the Congregational Church each Wednesday night and sang in the choir Sundays. Her voice was pleasant and everyone said it was a pleasure to hear her sing, but she didn't have any ambition vocally. The designing of costumes was what intrigued her.

"I loathed school and teachers and books," she used to say. "I would sit in class and scribble drawings in the margins of my books."

At seventeen she finished high school and went to study designing at Chicago's Academy of Fine Arts; six months later she had a job with a costume designer. One of her jobs took her to the Marigold Gardens, an old-time Chicago night club, and Ruth was assigned to design costumes for the chorus. The producer to whom she brought her drawings looked at the lissome, blue-eyed girl with the engaging smile and said, "How'd you like to go into show business?"

"Well . . . maybe I'd like it," Ruth stammered. "It might be fun."

So Ruth became a member of the line, dancing nightly in a costume which she designed. She was making $50 a week; $25 from the chorus and $25 as a designer. One night when she came to work she found the dressing rooms in a turmoil. The principal singer, a man, had taken sick suddenly and there was no one to go on in his place. The manager grabbed her.

"Can you sing?" he demanded.

"I guess so," Ruth said. And found herself hastily putting on white pants, white polo shirt and polo hat. With the chorus behind her and waving a polo mallet, she stood in the spotlight and sang "Hats Off to the Polo Girl."

"All I could think of was how terrible my feet must look," she said. "We had stuffed the toes so my feet would fit the ailing singer's shoes."

Ruth was now established as a star at the Marigold Gardens. Then the flu epidemic of 1918 hit Chicago and the cafés were ordered closed. She sold Christmas cards until the epidemic scare was over. It was at this time that she met "The Gimp" one night when he was backstage at the Marigold Gardens. He came from humble beginnings in Chicago's ghetto and had risen to a small political job, based (it was said) on his usefulness to the gangsters who ruled Chicago at that time. One of the seventeen bullets he was reputed to carry in his body had lamed him and earned him his unpleasant nickname.

Ruth was everything he wasn't, perhaps everything he wanted to be. She was an American of pioneer stock, beautiful, accomplished, healthy-minded, and admired and often loved by everyone she met. And The Gimp took one look and loved her too in his fashion. It was a love that was fierce and possessive to the point of making him slap anybody down who dared to "smile at my little lady." Years later when Ruth was in the Follies The Gimp worked himself into a rage because his little lady was paired with Helen Morgan in billing, and he marched up to Ziegfeld and warned him: 'You ain't gonna shove the little lady around even for a minute." Ziegfeld ordered him out of the theatre and made sure the order stuck. But The Gimp would wait out in the alley, smoking a cigar and pacing up and down as a kind of limping menace.

"Nobody's gonna shove us around," he would say. "The little lady don't need no Ziegfeld. One more crack out of him and I'll pull her outa the show."

The Gimp, at the time of their meeting, had good theatrical connections, being reputedly a bodyguard for Hal Halperin, the *Variety* man in Chicago, and often serving as volunteer protector for Al Jolson, Eddie Cantor and other actors when hoodlums tried to shake them down during Chicago visits. He used these connections for Ruth, her success became a mania with him, and he took great pride in being known as her manager and sole advisor. In him, love was synonymous with ferocity and Ruth said, years later, that when he proposed to her shortly after his divorce from his first wife she was too frightened to say anything but yes. They eloped to Crown Point, Indiana, on July 17, 1922. Whenever friends asked her how she put up with her husband's constant badgering she'd reply, "If I leave him, he'll kill me." About this time her husband changed his name from Moe to Martin (it seemed more distinguished for the husband of a future star) and added before it "Colonel," which had for years been another nickname and one, he thought, that added dignity. So he was now Colonel Martin Snyder and as such he spread his Svengali-like influence over Ruth, and for Ruth.

There began years of a steady, hectic rise to fame, for which Snyder, although his methods were crude, undoubtedly was partly responsible. He pounded desks, he wheedled, angled, cajoled and fought until her salary went from $25 to $2,500 a week. He made such a nuisance of himself that he was often barred from the clubs where Ruth was singing. He chose her friends, he made her engagements, he ruled her ruthlessly (the bitter pun is intended), insisting sometimes that she accept a singing role she didn't want. Nothing, however, could compensate Ruth for the unending drudgery, the drab living in hotel rooms, the constant fear of The Gimp's wrath. As she put it: "He fought with everyone and made my life miserable." She was never at any time allowed to enjoy the fruits of her success. Ruth wanted, above everything else, to shake free of the shackles of her marriage but she couldn't. She was afraid of The Gimp and even more afraid of leaving him. At the end of fifteen years she told him she couldn't take it any longer; she couldn't sing unless he freed her. Snyder agreed, possibly because he felt her success, which constituted his hold on her, would slip through his fingers if Ruth meant what she said. She sued Snyder for divorce on grounds of extreme cruelty and at the time of the settlement (for which he is supposed to have been given $100,000) he demanded her assurance that there was no other man in her life. There wasn't any. With The Gimp around, such a thing would have been impossible.

At the time of their divorce in November, 1937, there was no question of another man. True, Myrl Alderman had become Ruth's arranger and accompanist two years previously, but even the ferret eyes of The Gimp couldn't make anything out of this. After her Las Vegas divorce Ruth went on to Hollywood and Alderman quite naturally went with her. He was now in the process of getting a divorce from his second wife, Alma, who had recently presented him with a daughter. By California law he would not be free to marry again for one year. But when The Gimp heard that his "little lady" was seeing Alderman, he telephoned her from Chicago. "What do you mean running around with this guy when our divorce decree is hardly cold?" he asked. A few months later he came to Hollywood to inquire if the stories he heard of her marriage to Alderman were true. The Gimp brooded for several weeks until finally the jealous rage in his heart gave way to violence and he shot Alderman in his Hollywood Hills home. The bullet took a lucky course and Alderman lived to marry Ruth two months later while The Gimp was on trial. He served one year in prison, but Ruth by that time was happily married and in a retirement brought on after Alma Alderman sued Ruth for $150,000, charging her with alienating her husband's affections. The suit was dismissed but only after Ruth had been subjected to a great deal of damaging publicity.

The movie version of Ruth's life — *Love Me or Leave Me* — opened at the Music Hall in New York City on May 26, 1955. Doris Day proved her ability as an actress as well as a singer in her portrayal of Ruth, with James Cagney as The Gimp and Cameron Mitchell as Myrl Alderman.

Ruth made a brief comeback ten years ago. It had been a long, long time since she had worked for Ziegfeld but she still honored him as the greatest showman she had ever known. In an interview at the time she said of him, "There'll never be another like Ziegfeld. He employed such fine taste and sense of beauty in everything he did. He was a complete perfectionist, to the most minute detail, no matter what the cost.

"I remember one production over which artists, designers, and technicians labored for months to perfect. To everyone but him it seemed the costumes and sets couldn't be more gorgeous. His critical eye caught a few minor faults, so he ordered everything thrown out and done over to his satisfaction."

chapter nine

Empires struggle for ascendancy, reach a certain plateau of glory, and slip down the farther slope to decay and ruin. And so it is with the personal glory of men, excepting a few such as saints and philosophers who do not seek personal glory but to illuminate the ways of God. So it was with Florenz Ziegfeld. He was a supreme egotist and hence a lonely man, and for this reason also he could not give much of himself to anyone. He loved Billie Burke to the extent that his nature would permit, but he could not love her as much as she did him. He respected, as one man of talent respects another, Gene Buck, who wrote the lyrics for fifteen editions of the Follies and eighteen Midnight Frolics, and returned from an independent producing career to Ziegfeld in 1931 for the last Follies. On the other hand, Ziegfeld vastly underrated the ability of Ring Lardner and caused him weeks and years of frustrated bewilderment. Certainly he must have admired Oscar Hammerstein 2nd and Jerome Kern, who collaborated on the lyrics and music of "Ol' Man River," believed by many to be the greatest song in Ziegfeld's greatest production *Show Boat*. These were among the men who were associated with Ziegfeld in his Golden Age, and Buck, of course, came back to help him when that age was over and Ziegfeld was on that farther slope. I don't think it will be disputed that Buck was a foremost influence in shaping Ziegfeld's glory.

Buck was and is a man of many talents and his story has the fascination of an American folk tale. It is the poverty-to-fame fable with a different twist. Buck was born in Detroit, the son of an inventor — an occupation that is one of life's greatest gambles. The father died when the child was two years old and it is scarcely necessary to say he left the family impoverished. At eighteen, after two years in a Jesuit college, Buck went to work as a bank messenger at two dollars a week. It helped to hold off the wolf but it soon became evident that Buck was allergic to banks. He wanted to be an artist — it was more than a want, it was a compulsion — and he used to sketch on scraps of paper whenever he found the time. Charles Dana Gibson was his idol and his model. A paying teller looked at some of the sketches and advised young Buck to get out of the bank before he became immured in its routine. Buck looked around and jumped at a job with a manufacturing concern that made cover designs for sheet music. In those days music covers were stodgy and Buck suggested to the firm that they liven them up. To his astonishment and delight they agreed. His first covers were for "My Creole Belle" and "Hiawatha."

The young artist produced some 5,000 cover designs until something happened — ulcers, the doctor said — to the retina of his eyes and he went blind. He was blind for three desperate months, but he did not despair. In his darkness he thought hard about himself and what he wanted to do, and when his sight came back he said good-by to Detroit and set out for New York. He found work in his trade to keep him going, but at the same time, in a studio next to that of James Montgomery Flagg, he began to draw what he wanted to draw, with no concern whether or not it would sell. He also began to write jingles and jokes for the comic weeklies. And that brought him to the decision to become a lyricist. He found a composer, Dave Stamper, who was willing to take a chance, and their first song, "Daddy Has a Sweetheart and Mother Is Her Name" was bought by Ziegfeld for his 1911 Follies.

If you suppose this opened the door to success you are mistaken. A. L. Erlanger owned a considerable piece of the show, and Erlanger did not think much of Lillian Lorraine, who was delegated to sing the song. Result: the song left the show, followed in short order by Lillian. But she did sing it at the elder Oscar Hammerstein's Victoria vaudeville theatre and she put it over so well it sold close to a million copies.

The Buck-Stamper team followed this with "Some Boy" and it was not long after that Buck put away his drawing board and went to work for Ziegfeld. He became much more than a lyricist. He helped to whip the shows into shape and he had an uncanny instinct for new talent. He spotted Ed Wynn in a Brooklyn vaudeville house, he came upon Will Rogers in the same variety medium, he heard John Steel as a Y.M.C.A. secretary with a church choir, he found Frisco dancing in a Chicago basement, he watched W. C. Fields juggling — and he roped them all in for the Follies. His proudest discovery, he has said, was Joseph Urban. Urban had come to America to design scenery for the Russell Opera Company of Boston just as that company was staggering toward collapse. So he was engaged to paint the sets for something called *The Garden of Paradise*. It was a hellish flop. But Buck

INTERNATIONAL NEWS PHOTOS, INC.

Ring Lardner who wrote lyrics for Ziegfeld

knew talent when he saw it. He insisted on Ziegfeld accompanying him to the Park Theatre and Ziegfeld dubiously gave way to persuasion and engaged the great designer for the Follies. In his days with Ziegfeld, Buck collaborated with such top composers as Victor Herbert, Kern, Rudolph Friml, Louis Hirsch and James Hanley. He went on to become president of the American Society of Composers, Authors and Publishers (ASCAP), and to become also one of the great names in and out of the entertainment world.

The association of Ring Lardner and Ziegfeld was an off-and-on affair and illustrates how Ziegfeld could miss once in a while. If Jove occasionally nods, Ziegfeld occasionally snored. Lardner became enchanted by the Follies when, as a young newspaperman in Chicago, he saw the first edition in 1907. He also became a saloon companion and then a friend of Bert Williams. Lardner began trying to write songs for Williams, with the latter's encouragement and praise, but they weren't much good and Ziegfeld junked them. It was not until 1917 that Lardner's name appeared on a Follies program as the author of "Home, Sweet Home (That's Where the Real War Is)," sung by Williams.

When the Follies of 1922 was in preparation Lardner thought he had really made it. He was engaged with Ralph Spence to write the book. This was the show that had in it Gilda Gray, goddess of the "shimmy," Gallagher and Shean, and was topped by Will Rogers. Three of the sketches Lardner wrote were dropped entirely and the other two subjected to interpolation and rewriting. Even collaboration with Buck failed to break the curse on Lardner's work – which probably was based on a complete lack of understanding between him and Ziegfeld. They were not *simpatico*. But Lardner kept on trying. In late 1930 when *Smiles* went into rehearsal the book was by William Anthony McGuire, music by Vincent Youmans, and lyrics by Clifford Grey and Harold Afamson. This was Ziegfeld's time of desperation and it might have been this impending sense of doom that led him to ask Lardner to write some more lyrics. The show featured Marilyn Miller and the As-

PICTURE COLLECTION, NEW YORK PUBLIC LIBRARY

Gilda Gray

PICTURE COLLECTION, NEW YORK PUBLIC LIBRARY

Gilda Gray, originator of the "Shimmie"

taires, and the Boston tryout opening put it in the category of a frantic failure. Despite revisions, it died dismally in New York after 63 performances.

Years before, after Lardner's experience with the Follies of 1922, he wrote "A Day with Conrad Green." To friends Lardner said the character of Conrad Green was based on that of Ziegfeld. It is a savage little tale, depicting Conrad Green as an egomaniac and a petty tyrant, with no consideration for his wife, mistress, or employees, and no humanity whatever, a thief of other men's ideas, a hypocrite and a liar. It is an attack with a bludgeon instead of a knife and it suggests that Lardner was writing out of his own furious frustration of ever becoming a Follies great. The best way to wrap up the Ziegfeld-Lardner relationship is to repeat that they were not *simpatico,* and they never could be. Lardner at his best was a magnificent satirist, Ziegfeld at his best was a great glorifier, and the two could never meet.

In the evening of his Golden Age, but while it still was golden, Ziegfeld continued to live in the manner of a grandee. It is not worth trying here to poke around amateurishly into the subconscious, but it seems to me he was forced to live that way not only because of the ruts of habit, but because that way of living was the crowning justification of his career. Ziegfeld measured things by outward symbols, of which the most important were wealth and its ostentatious habiliments. He had very little inner life in the spiritual and philosophic sense, and he was always a stranger to serenity. His Follies, because of rising costs, were reaching the financial state of no return. In 1927, for example, costumes for the Follies cost $123,000, not including a shipment of tights from Paris for his girls at a price of $2,329. The total cost before the show opened and before a seat was sold was $289,000, and the salaries of his stars were up as high as $5,000 a week.

The Burkely Crest estate also was an essential symbol. There Ziegfeld used to be host to a large number of personages on week ends, not caring much who they were so long as they were personages. It cost $10,000 a month to operate. In addition to the magnetic attraction of the gaming tables, Ziegfeld was heavily committed in the stock market. But this was before 1929, when the world was a bright and marvelous playground for those, like Ziegfeld, who knew precisely how to balance the bars and the exact amount of leverage to apply to the seesaws, or thrust to the soaring swings, and everything was going to be all right. It had to be to those who knew.

Then came '29 and the crash, and the evening of the Golden Age turned suddenly into night. Miss Burke relates that Ziegfeld broke into tears. They were childish tears. Some huge, impersonal, cruel force had smashed his infinitely precious symbols.

Ziegfeld was not finished—men of his type are not finished easily—but this was a period of extreme shock, of stunned daylight hours devoted to the automatic mechanisms of living, and of restless, tortured nights. In such a time a man's mind turns back on itself, partly as a defense against facing the realities of the present, and in a fitful, dreaming fashion fastens on past successes and on the persons who contributed to them — or rather, as an egotist would place them, the persons whom he chose as supernumeraries in those successes. Such mental meanderings, I would imagine, have a hallucinatory quality; that is, they have no relation to the sequence of the years — an event or personality of prominence, let us say in 1912, might be juxtaposed with an event or personality in 1926. In dreams time is more of a whirlpool than a river. Chronology does not exist. And so — I am candidly conjecturing now — in this period of shock the figures of the principals who added to his achievements, and more particularly the girls he glorified (for after all they were the hallmark of his fame), must have flitted through his memory: the beautiful and triumphant, the beautiful and lost. There are a number of such girls who would flash into the patchwork fabric of his dreams. Here are some we haven't described as yet.

Mae Murray, for instance, she of the bee-stung lips, piquant profile, felicitous feet — 96 pounds of lovely litheness. She started her climb to world fame and wealth as a dancer in the Follies. Mae was the original Nell Brinkley girl, of the drawings that delicately provoked the desire of men and aroused the envy of women of that era. Merry Murray, with her blonde curls and perfectly formed tiny body, conveyed the impression that she was not earthbound like other mortals but could, at will, fly away at any moment in a twinkling visit to the Milky Way.

Mae Murray at home.

PICTURE COLLECTION, NEW YORK PUBLIC LIBRARY

INTERNATIONAL NEWS PHOTOS, INC.

Mae Murray in Ziegfeld Follies of 1920

INTERNATIONAL NEWS PHOTOS, INC.
Mae Murray arrives from Europe – 1925

She danced her way up to New York's Sans Souci and a feature part with Irene and Vernon Castle in Charles Dillingham's *Watch Your Step*. She left Ziegfeld, she said, only "after I had reached the top in the Follies and could go no further." The movies eagerly gave her the chance to extend her journeying. She made the picture *The Merry Widow* with John Gilbert, the Hollywood idol who cast a swoonlike charm over women, and her name is still synonymous with the picture. Miss Murray married a millionaire's son, W. N. Schwenker, Jr. Her second husband was Jay O'Brien, New York socialite; her third, Robert Z. Leonard, celebrated movie director; and her fourth, Prince David Mdivani, a member of the blond trio of princes whose wives included Barbara Hutton, Newport's Louise Van Alen, Pola Negri and Mary McCormick. She was indeed Ziegfeld's pocket-size Venus.

Blonde, blue-eyed Marion Davies was discovered by Ziegfeld when she was dancing in the chorus of *Oh Boy!* the year after she made her first professional appearance, also in the chorus, in *Chu Chin Chow*. She was entrancing, with the appeal of a Dresden china doll. Her beauty also attracted the admiration of two famous artists, Howard Chandler Christy and Harrison Fisher, who portrayed her on many canvases (she was the model for Fisher's immensely popular "Morning"). Marion also graduated from the Follies to the films, and almost overnight established herself as one of Hollywood's sweetest of sweet youg things. But Miss Davies had a great deal more than that. It has been said she was a "natural" comedienne. Certainly she had an incomparable sense of humor. But there is no such phenomenon as a "natural" comedienne, professionally speaking. Marion had the natural ability but she had to work hard to acquire the sheen that characterized her later performances.

Among the beautiful and lost was Hilda Ferguson, a blonde from Baltimore, with a tiny rosebud mouth, a turned-up nose, big eyes and a seductive body, who in her tempestuously alcoholic career was the sweetheart (mistress is too formal a word for Hilda) of gangsters, actors, politicians and financiers. Hilda drank an incredible amount of straight gin and occasionally, in deference to convention, champagne — but gin was her passenger. She also displayed in the sensational episodes of her life the tight-lipped silence that is considered a mark of sterling character in the underworld.

The first such episode was the unsolved murder of Dot King, who was found chloroformed in her New York apartment in 1923. Hilda was then shimmying in the Follies in a costume of silver strands that disclosed more than they hid, and she also shared Dot King's apartment. Hilda shrugged off police interrogation by insisting she hadn't been home for a week and knew nothing of motives, circumstances or likely suspects. Again in 1931 she was the companion of "Tough Willie" McCabe, bodyguard of notorious Arnold Rothstein. When McCabe was slugged and stabbed in the 61 Club, Hilda again knew nothing and got off a historic remark in New York's General Sessions Court. "My dear," she said to General Sessions Judge Freschi, "I was in the ladies' room at the time." Judge Freschi, after digesting Hilda's fond greeting incredulously, answered, "It is very nice to be called 'my dear' but I don't know whether I like it or not in these circumstances." Hilda "jumped" the Follies when the King inquiry was hot and disappeared for two months, and in the McCabe case she forfeited $5,000 bail. Again, in a state investigation into the activities of a top politician in Atlantic City, New Jersey, who had backed Hilda in a lavish night club venture, Hilda again refused to testify.

Then Hilda really fell in love. The man was not rich. He was not famous. He was a nice guy who adored her and asked her to marry him. "Me? He wants to marry me?" Hilda thought and it cut her to the heart. Hilda poured her gin down the drain and went on the wagon. "He doesn't want me to be a lady," she told Jack Lait, one of the greatest of Broadway reporters, "but he does want me to be a woman, and I'll make it or die in the attempt." She did die in the attempt, of peritonitis a month later at the age of thirty, and was buried in an inexpensive grave in the city of her birth.

INTERNATIONAL NEWS PHOTOS, INC.

Hilda Ferguson

Hope Dare
INTERNATIONAL NEWS PHOTOS, INC.

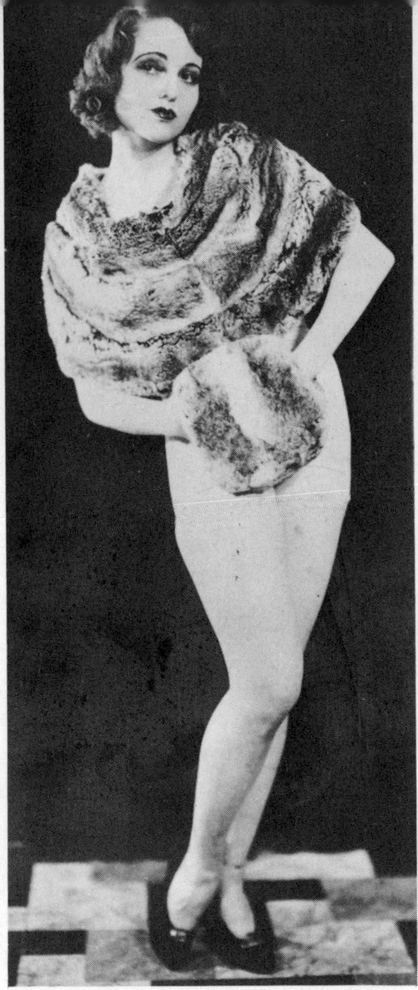
Hope Dare
INTERNATIONAL NEWS PHOTOS, INC.

Hope Dare would have been just another dime-a-dozen pretty girl if she hadn't become intimately and dangerously involved with the Dutch Schultz gang in New York by becoming the mistress and later the wife of Julius Richard (Dixie) Davis, the diminutive lawyer with the shrewd, facile, ambitious mind who was the brains behind the toughest mob in America at that time.

She was born Rosie Lutzinger in Fairfield, Iowa, and she was ambitious too. She studied dancing. At seventeen she married a Los Angeles newspaper promoter who was forty; she was named "Miss Southern California" in a Los Angeles bathing-beauty contest; and on the death of her husband, overcoming her widow's grief in a short time, arrived in New York as Rose Dare, which she changed to Hope Dare when she made the Follies. It was at this point that Davis, who now was rolling in wealth, saw her and installed her in a penthouse. He was married, but that was a minor technicality.

The life magnificent ended when Schultz was chopped down by bullets

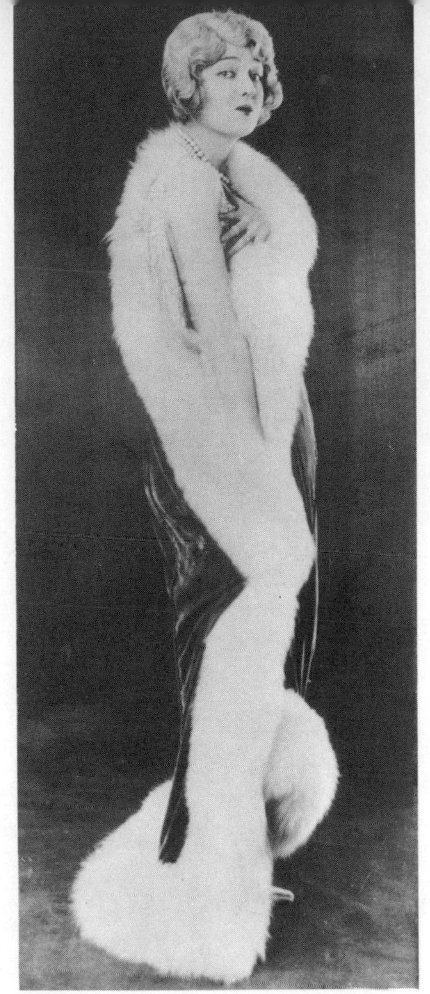

INTERNATIONAL NEWS PHOTOS, INC.

Peggy Hopkins Joyce

INTERNATIONAL NEWS PHOTOS, INC.

Peggy Hopkins Joyce

in a Newark chophouse in 1935 and then began days of flight and fear, for Hope knew too much and gangsters don't approve of people who know too much. She was joined by Davis but the law caught up with them eventually in a West Philadelphia apartment. Davis was sentenced to serve a year and Hope waited for him, for this, as they said, was "a deathless love." His wife divorced him during his imprisonment, and when he was freed he and Hope were married and went West. The deathless love that survived violence and dread did not survive the calmer seas of matrimony, and ended in deathless divorce after a year or two.

There are many other glorious girls, some famous, some a memory to only a few, some successful, some destined for early death, who may well have entered as fragments into Ziegfeld's patchwork of dreams. . . .

Peggy Hopkins Joyce, chiefly notable for her unquenchable enthusiasm for matrimony. . . .

INTERNATIONAL NEWS PHOTOS, INC.

Peggy Fears

Another Peggy, this one named Fears, who came to New York and the Follies by way of New Orleans and Dallas and who was introduced by Charlie Chaplin to Alfred Cleveland Blumenthal, known to intimates as Blumey, whom she married in 1927. Blumey was a Broadway angel, a genial host of lavish parties, and an intimate friend of Jimmy Walker, New York's ebullient mayor. Divorce ended this romance. . . .

Christine Conniff, Danbury, Connecticut — a dark-haired and dark-eyed girl who graced *Kid Boots, Comic Supplement* (one of the few Ziegfeld flops) and *Sunny*. She died at the height of her loveliness. . . .

Lina Basquette, a vivacious brunette who became the wife of movie mogul Sam Warner, then of Peverell Marley, who later married Linda Darnell, then of Teddy Hayes, one-time trainer for Jack Dempsey, then of Evelyn Mollison, British actor. . . .

Gladys Feldman, who married Horace Braham, insurance executive, and who now is president of the Ziegfeld Club, which is a great deal more than a group of kindred spirits since it is devoted to the welfare of former Ziegfeld girls. . . .

INTERNATIONAL NEWS PHOTOS, INC.

Lina Basquette of the 1925 Follies being serenaded backstage on her engagement to Sam Warner, movie producer.

Gladys Feldman

PICTURE COLLECTION,
NEW YORK PUBLIC LIBRARY

THE ZIEGFELD CLUB

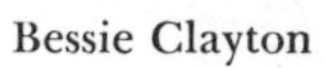

Bessie Clayton

INTERNATIONAL NEWS PHOTOS, INC.

Lina Basquette – a publicity shot

Anastasia Reilly

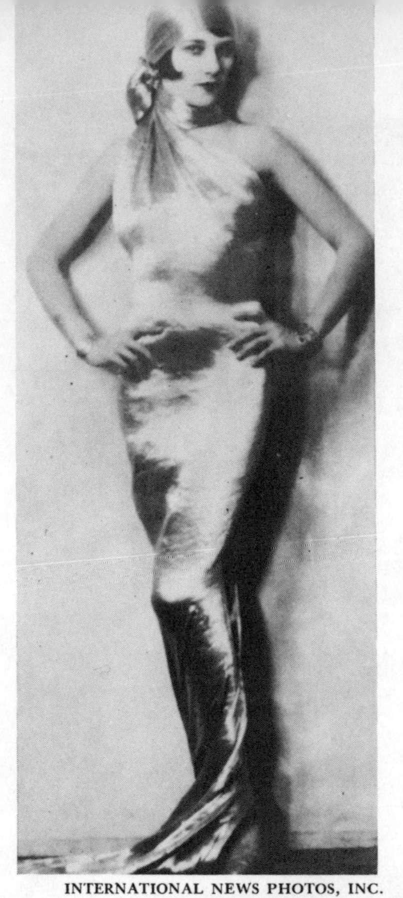

INTERNATIONAL NEWS PHOTOS, INC.

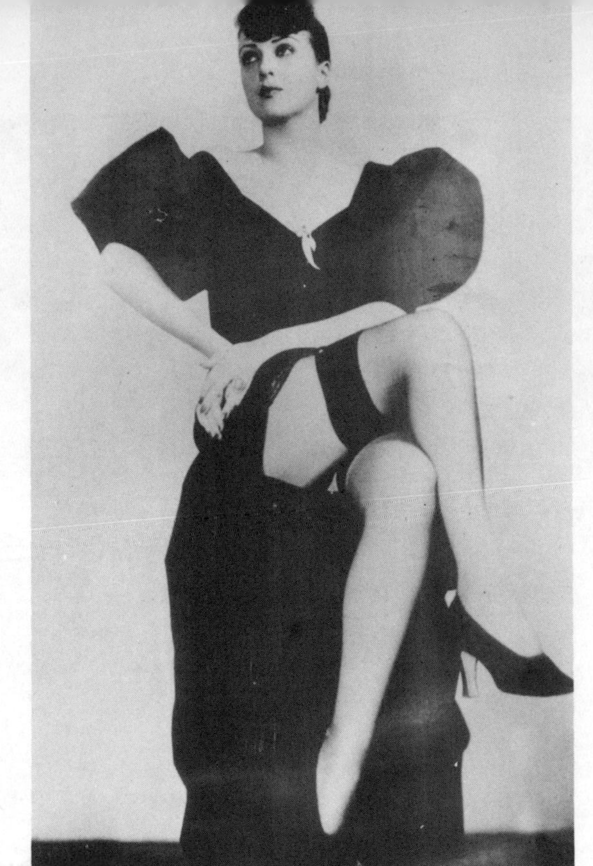

INTERNATIONAL NEWS PHOTOS, INC.

Gypsy Rose Lee

Gypsy Rose Lee, who you might say has stripped life to its essence. Is further identification necessary? . . .

Anastasia Reilly, the "dream girl" of the mid-twenties. The dreams she evoked among males are better intimated than explicitly described. . . .

Jose Collins, the English girl who was in the Follies from 1911 to 1917 and found it a road to the peerage. She married Lord Robert Innes-Ker, uncle of the Duke of Roxburghe. She was bankrupt in 1926 and a year later found herself the recipient of a $100,000-a-year income due to the thoughtfulness of Frank Curzon, of race-track fame, who bequeathed her that amount in his will. Jose and her lord were divorced in 1935. . . .

Flo Leeds, a leading and sensational figure in the divorce proceedings involving banking tycoon Stillman in the 1920's. . . .

Bobbie Storey, an English girl, who committed suicide in an architect's apartment in New York in 1930. . . .

Allyn King, understudy in the Follies to Ina Claire. She was also a suicide. . . .

Martha Mansfield, burned to death in a fire caused by a carelessly flipped cigarette. . . .

Dorothy Dell, killed in an automobile accident. . . .

Ruby Keeler, who married the great Al Jolson, about the only great comedian and singer of the day who never appeared in the Follies. . . .

Hazel Forbes, who inherited millions from her husband and was married again to Harry Richman. . . .

Mary Eaton, a newspaperman's daughter, became a child actress in stock when she was thirteeen and traveled on from Washington to New York to become a top dancer in the Follies from 1923 to '30. Mary also starred in *Kid Boots* with Eddie Cantor. One of her greatest feats was to take the place of Marilyn Miller in *Sally* – with only one rehearsal – once when Marilyn was ill. She got into a quarrel with Ziegfeld when he demanded an insertion in her contract in which she would agree not to marry. Miss Eaton said "No" firmly, loudly, quietly and insistently, and Ziegfeld finally capitulated and removed the offensively virginal clause. . . . She died in Hollywood in 1948. . . .

Florence Leeds

INTERNATIONAL NEWS PHOTOS, INC.

INTERNATIONAL NEWS PHOTOS, INC.

Ruby Keeler, the Ziegfeld girl who married Al Jolson.

INTERNATIONAL NEWS PHOTOS, INC.

Sophie Tucker

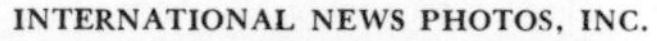

Mary Mulhern, Jack Pickford's last wife.

INTERNATIONAL NEWS PHOTOS, INC.

Katherine Burke

INTERNATIONAL NEWS PHOTOS, INC.

Sophie Tucker, who started her career singing for nickels and dimes in her parents' restaurant in Hartford at which the most famous dish was her mother's homemade gefüllte fish, appeared in the Follies of 1909. This was long, long before Sophie became known as the original Red Hot Mama and went on to fame. . . .

Barbara Stanwyck rose from the Ziegfeld chorus to become an enduring star, married Frank Fay, and then Robert Taylor. . . .

Cynthia Cambridge, once known as "Miss England," was thrown to her death when her horse bolted in Hyde Park. . . .

Cynthia's best friend, Peggy Shannon — the two entered the Follies together — was found dead at a kitchen table in North Hollywood, a half-smoked cigarette between her fingers. . . .

Helen Walsh burned to death in a fire on Harry Richman's yacht. . . .

Mary Alice Rice, a Temple University graduate, left Austin, Texas, to come to New York. She appeared in the last edition of the Follies and was one of the 12 girls selected out of 75 which formed The Golden Dozen. Ziegfeld called them the most beautiful girls on an American stage. Still slim, blond and lovely, Mary Alice is the fashion director for New York's Plaza and Ambassador hotels. . . .

Most of these girls belonged to an era that was naïvely exhibitionistic. To have, for example, only one diamond bracelet was regarded as a mark of inferiority and a certain indication that the one-bracelet girl either wasn't trying, or didn't have sufficient charm to arouse more than passing interest of a millionaire. To escape this social stigma some of the one-bracelet girls bought a couple of cut-glass bracelets and wore them with a brave-comic-sad show of pretension along with the authentic one. It sounds fantastic these days, but we have our foolish foibles, too.

These girls flashed and faded in that long stretch of years that marked Ziegfeld's rise and fall. He recovered from the shock of the Wall Street debacle, in which he lost a million dollars, and fiercely tried to come back. But his number was up. In this situation Billie Burke displayed her courage and love once more. Her earnings on the stage and screen had been more than considerable and she had had the good sense to seek out wise financial counseling, with the result that investments in bonds and government securities had accumulated in her name a reserve of $500,000, more than enough to insure her security and that of her beloved daughter, Patricia. But when her husband was knocked onto the ropes by the crash, Miss Burke was faced with a hard decision, and she made it instantly. She turned over all her money to Ziegfeld. It was merely a road block against immediate disaster, and no more.

Ziegfeld resumed his accustomed way of life — it was inevitable that he would, for now that way had become a desperate gesture of defiance against fate. He dictated completely unnecessary 500-word telegrams. He became

THE ZIEGFELD CLUB

Jocelyn Leigh

Olive Osborne

THE ZIEGFELD CLUB

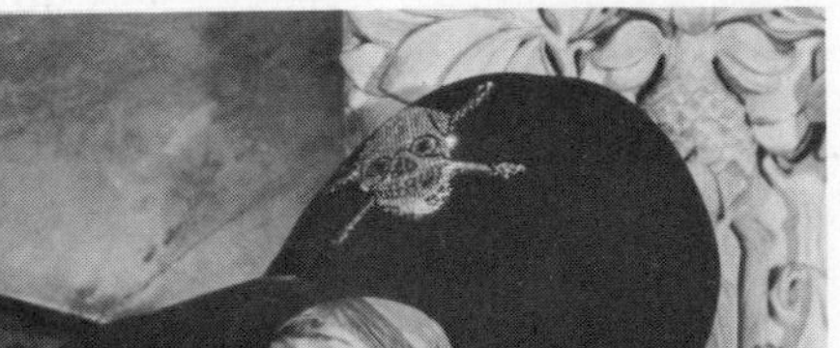

THEATRE COLLECTION, NEW YORK PUBLIC LIBRARY

Gladys Glad

the telephone company's most cherished client. He had to have his daily fresh-cut flowers, his Parisian cologne, his expensive clothes. One of his employees shook his head in bewilderment over a telegram running into hundreds of words and ending, I WILL WIRE YOU IN DETAIL LATER. While his last show, *Hot Cha!*, was trying out in Pittsburgh, Ziegfeld, standing in the rear of the theatre, dictated a long telegram to Lew Brown ordering changes in the first act. Brown, of course, was in the theatre at the time. Later, leaving the theatre, Ziegfeld met Brown in the lobby. He said good night and walked on. When Brown received the telegram a little while later, it was delivered to his hotel room, which was on the same floor as Ziegfeld's suite.

Thus did Ziegfeld try to fight off doom and hang on to the years and the tastes that were sinking into the quicksand of oblivion. The Burkely Crest estate had been mortgaged to the hilt. *Smiles* began to teeter on the edge of failure when Vincent Youmans tried to take his music out of it and was held back only when Ziegfeld went to court and obtained a restraining order. The show went into the red more than $300,000. Ziegfeld also was harassed by lawsuits. One was for $17,000 in back costume bills; another for $1,000 for flowers which Ziegfeld had sent not only to his wife but to Lili Damita and Gladys Glad. But he could be astonishingly considerate in his time of trouble, too. Eddie Cantor went to Hollywood with Ziegfeld's approval and encouragement. Ziegfeld went further. He turned over Cantor's contract to Sam Goydwyn and wished him godspeed. Ziegfeld relinquished his contractual hold on a great star because he sensed that Cantor's future was in the studios out West.

Show Girl, which opened at the Ziegfeld Theatre July 2, 1929, seemed to "have everything" to assure its success. There was a cast headed by Clayton, Jackson & Durante, Frank McHugh, Eddie Foy, Jr., Harriet Hoctor and Ruby Keeler (with unofficial down-the-aisle appearances by Al Jolson singing "Liza" while his wife Ruby was tap dancing on stage). There was a Gershwin score, a J. P. McEvoy book, and the dances were staged by Bobby Connelly and Albertina Rasch. But in spite of everything, the production was a box-office failure.

Ziegfeld decided to put on another edition of the Follies, that of 1931. Judged by the talent that went into it, it should have been a success. The music and sketches were by such gifted men as Gene Buck, Mark Hellinger, Walter Donaldson, Dave Stamper, Dr. Hugo Riesenfeld, Mack Gordon, Harry Revel and Dimitri Tiomkin. The scenery was by Joseph Urban, and in the cast were Gladys Glad (the great love of Hellinger's life), Faith Bacon, Harry Richman, Helen Morgan, Jack Pearl, Earle Oxford, Milton Le Roy, Hal Le Roy, Ruth Etting, the Collette Sisters, Dorothy Dell, Mitzi Mayfair, Billie Seward. It should have been a success, but it wasn't despite the tremendous effort that went into it. The reason was that the Follies formula had become old-fashioned. It all began to seem passé, "and to tell the truth, my dear, a little dull" — a fact that Ziegfeld would not or could not recognize. (The fact was proved again when a 1956 imitation Follies with Tallulah Bankhead closed on the road recently). He was a man trying to go home again, to the great glamorous home he had built himself, and, alas, it was beyond even hope of repair.

There remained *Hot Cha!*, which had in it Lupe Velez, that sensual gamin, and Bert Lahr, that zany comedian, certainly one of the greatest in his trade. Lupe had started her professional career in Mexico City as a dancer when she was thirteen, and went on to Hollywood to play with Douglas Fairbanks, Sr. in *The Gaucho*. When Ziegfeld grabbed her in 1932 for *Hot Cha!*, Lupe's career was hot, too. Later she died of an overdose of sleeping pills in Beverly Hills. Ziegfeld fell ill of influenza while directing the production in Pittsburgh, and the flu turned into pneumonia when the show moved into New York. He virtually directed it from his bed in the Warwick Hotel, across from the Ziegfeld Theatre, and was sick and on the verge of coma when it opened. Nevertheless, he summoned his iron will and listened to it by radio attachment to the theatre. This was a bad year generally for the theatre, and it was a worse one for Ziegfeld, who was not only sick physically but on the thin edge of nervous collapse. He literally was driving himself toward death. But he would not give up. Perhaps if he had given up, he would have died sooner and in shame. Who is qualified to say?

Ziegfeld turned that year to radio. The magic of his name and the awe of the Ziegfeld touch were still strong. He put on a Sunday afternoon show for Chrysler Motors and he did it with the typical Ziegfeldian grandeur and sweep. He drafted Al Goodman, who had become musical director for the Follies, and built the show around Jane Froman, Art Jarrett and Jack Pearl. It was, if you like, a potpourri, or perhaps a bouillabaisse, of scenes, music and stars, for Ziegfeld, despite the success of both *Show Boat* productions (he staged a revival in 1932), was still suspicious of plots. But something new was added. Ziegfeld emerged from his former backstage, or back-of-the-theatre, aloofness and appeared as part of the show. He was not, of course, an entertainer, but he made a three-minute commentary kickoff of the show. He faltered and hemmed and hawed at first, but soon he gained confidence and with confidence began to enjoy it. Maybe he asked himself: How long has this been going on?

But Ziegfeld was a sick man and Billy Burke, working hard on the West Coast, finally discovered it by a little slip in his voice in one of the broadcasts she listened to each Sunday. She and her husband had been in communication by way of typical Ziegfeldian telegrams and long-distance calls but he had concealed his condition by resolute cheerfulness and assurance. That little break in his voice ended the brave deception and alarmed Miss Burke so much that she succeeded in closing out a play which was in the tryout stage. A few days before, she had signed a contract with David O. Selznick,

INTERNATIONAL NEWS PHOTOS, INC.

Bert Lahr and Lupe Velez

at the instance of her true friend George Cukor, to appear with John Barrymore and Katherine Hepburn, then a new find for the movies, in *A Bill of Divorcement.* This picture was to be made a few months hence, so Miss Burke left for New York, secure at least in the knowledge that she and her husband would have something to fall back on if the worse came to the worst.

Miss Burke began to plot with devoted deception. She evolved no master plan, the way a general staff would do, or even a sequence of strategy, but she knew that she had to help her husband in this hour of his blackest need and she played it, as the saying goes, by ear, using her woman's subtlety and intuition to meet each development as it came. The first thing, of course, was to get to New York and to make it seem an impulsive visit undertaken as a loving whim. So she packed and traveled, and when she saw her husband and embraced him, she hid in her heart the shock of his appearance. He was thin and pale. His strength had been drained out of him by fatigue and illness and he held himself erect with the forced, feeble and obvious effort of an old man. But Ziegfeld put on a semblance of gaiety and Miss Burke went along with it. They laughed and joked and exchanged endearments and did the town after a fashion. It wasn't too bad when they were among acquaintances but when they were alone together at Burkely Crest not all the pretense they could summon could bestow the warmth of by-gone days to the now dismal rooms or to the gardens that took on to Miss Burke the fevered brightness of decay. One evening Ziegfeld sagged and slumped on the table in a hotel dining room as they were listening to the lilting music of Buddy Rogers' band, and Miss Burke knew she had crossed into another phase of caring for him.

She knew also her husband's tremendous and vulnerable pride. So a day or two later she quietly journeyed by herself to New York from the Yonkers estate, bought tickets for California and obtained permission for her husband to board the train at Harmon, New York, not far from Yonkers, a locomotive junction point. Only a handful of persons knew of the arrangements, among them Kathryn Dix, Ziegfeld's loyal secretary.

Ziegfeld was too weak to put up more than token resistance. It was midsummer of 1932, and humidly hot. Miss Burke tried to comfort him by putting under his head pillowcases packed with crushed ice. It is doubtful if Ziegfeld, at the beginning of that trip West, had more than a vague idea of what was going on, and at intervals when he tried to dictate telegrams, imagining, perhaps, that he was in his office, he had no idea at all. That was a dreadful journey. Miss Burke had him taken from the train at Barstow, California, where there was little chance of their being recognized, and sped him to her Santa Monica home, where she successfully hid him from the world.

There, amid peace and beauty and the love of his wife and daughter, Ziegfeld's mind grew clearer; he was able to sit up and then to walk around the house and garden, and Miss Burke prayed that he was on the road to recovery. In fact, she wept for joy when his profligate habits returned. For Ziegfeld, with resurgent confidence, was planning to return to his radio show in New York and wanted to be close to his revival of *Show Boat*. He thought it was a smash success and Miss Burke did not tell him it was becoming financially ruinous, as all the profits had to be siphoned off to clamoring creditors. He resumed his costly long-distance calls and his telephone bill for one month alone was $6,000. But not even Ziegfeld's magnificent egotism and resourcefulness could beat this one. His intelligence was functioning but he was too sick and weak. Death was standing in the doorway . . . awaiting the cue.

Miss Burke was driven by the fear that was gnawing at her all the time to summon physicians. They advised that Ziegfeld be taken to a hospital. He agreed without much fuss, in the belief that this was merely to be a checkup with a week or two of professional observation and care. Miss Burke took a room in the hospital next to his, and traveled daily from there to work in *Bill of Divorcement*. It was a case of absolute financial necessity now, and she was frightened because it was her first talking picture. George Cukor helped her to overcome her nervousness and John Barrymore's friendly genius carried her over the first few scenes. Midway or so in the

Costumes for the Follies of 1918

PICTURE COLLECTION, NEW YORK PUBLIC LIBRARY

The Line-Up. Follies of 1922

THE ZIEGFELD CLUB

Bird Number from the Ziegfeld *Midnight Frolic* – 1925. Setting by Joseph Urban

THE ZIEGFELD CLUB

picture, Miss Burke was told she wouldn't be needed for perhaps ten days since scenes were scheduled in which she did not appear. She was jubilant. This was a certain sign of good fortune, she thought, for now she could be with her husband constantly, and he seemed cheerful and at last on the long climb back to health. Everything, she told herself, was going to be all right.

The first day of her leisure was July 22 and it was wonderful . . . until late afternoon. Miss Burke had breakfast with her husband, and their daughter Patty brought a lunch she had prepared at home. It was relaxed and intimate, as only a family group can be. Then in the afternoon, the movie business being what it is, Miss Burke received a call from the studio. They were very sorry, but it was a matter of urgency. Could Miss Burke make an evening test with an actor who was being considered for a part in the picture? His name, by the way, was Walter Pidgeon, and he didn't quite make it for the part — that is the way the movies are, too. Miss Burke sighed and said of course.

She went to the studio after having dinner with Ziegfeld and got into her

Ben Ali Haggin tableau of 1923 — "The Triumph of Love"

INTERNATIONAL NEWS PHOTOS, INC.

Ben Ali Haggin at a Beaux Arts Ball

The famous Haggin tableau, "A Kiss In the Dark" — before

THE ZIEGFELD CLUB

"A Kiss In the Dark" — after

THE ZIEGFELD CLUB

THE ZIEGFELD CLUB

ALFRED CHENEY JOHNSTON — THE ZIEGFELD CLUB

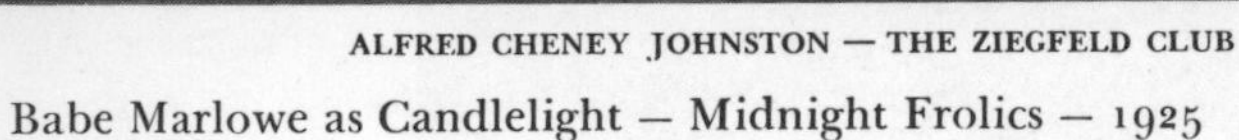

Babe Marlowe as Candlelight — Midnight Frolics — 1925

ALFRED CHENEY JOHNSTON — THE ZIEGFELD CLUB

Emily Drange as Lanternlight — Midnight Frolics — 1925

make-up and costume, heavy mascara and a long evening gown. She and Pidgeon rehearsed the scene and were about to go before the cameras when the hospital telephoned.

It was essential for Miss Burke to come at once. Did she understand? At once!

Miss Burke gathered up her gown, raced out of the studio and hurled herself into a car. She pleaded with the driver to go faster — faster. At the same moment, Patty was also on the way from the Burke home. Miss Burke rushed into the hospital and into her husband's room. One look at the terribly still body and the closed eyes of the white, thin face told her the story. She was, she learned later, precisely two minutes late. A heart attack does not take very long. Strong hands held her and voices spoke to her but she did not hear them. She returned to reality lying on a bed, her face streaked with mascara and nurses trying to remove her drawing-room comedy gown. Within a few minutes newspaper presses throughout the nation and much

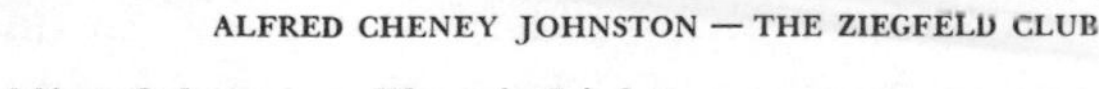

ALFRED CHENEY JOHNSTON — THE ZIEGFELD CLUB

ALFRED CHENEY JOHNSTON — THE ZIEGFELD CLUB

Olive Osborne as Electric Light — Gladys Loftus as Sunlight — Midnight Frolics — 1925

of the rest of the world were roaring out headlines: ZIEGFELD DIES AT 63, GREAT PRODUCER PASSES.

So this was the end. Patricia arrived some twenty minutes after her mother, and the two clung together in grief. Presently Will Rogers and his wife came and led them gently away.

Ziegfeld made many enemies in his career and also made strong and loyal friends. Among the former were George White and Earl Carroll, his competitors in the glorifying game, whom he scorned. Once when he entered a night club with a party the band was playing a medley from Carroll's Vanities. Ziegfeld did an about-face and stalked out, his party trailing behind. He and George M. Cohan also were mutually hostile and Cohan would not allow a tune from any Ziegfeld show to be played in any theatre in which he was appearing.

Among the friends none was more loyal or understanding than Will

Rogers. He took Miss Burke and Patty to his home and kept them secluded there. There were some who wanted a big, gaudy, garish funeral for Ziegfeld in New York, but Miss Burke and Will Rogers said no. Rogers took charge of the arrangements and a quiet, private funeral was held in Hollywood. In his capsule column the following day in *The New York Times,* Rogers wrote: "Goodbye Flo, save a spot for me. You will put on a show up there someday that will knock their eye out."

Days of stunned languor followed for Miss Burke, but they could not last. They could not last because of the demands life was making upon her, and because she was obliged by her character not to evade these demands but to meet them head on as best she could. Ziegfeld's estate, for instance, consisted of at least $500,000 in debts. Six creditor suits were launched almost immediately. Some time later, Ziegfeld's office safe was opened. It contained eleven unused rubber bands; two five-dollar bills, series 1928; copies of three songs written for the 1915, '19 and '25 Follies; a tin brooch with a large glass ruby; an Oriental silk elephant whip with a jeweled handle; and a small, bronze-black elephant, his talisman against misfortune.

Burkely Crest, of course, had been a white elephant of bad luck. Eventually, this big estate, which had cost $250,000, was sold at auction for $36,000, and its furnishings, consisting of 295 objects which had cost $35,000, went under the hammer for $6,000. An ornate walnut bed made to order for Ziegfeld, and beside which he kept three telephones, brought $31. The one sentimental touch in this hard bargaining dismemberment of worldly glory was the purchase by Lew Brown, producer of several Ziegfeld shows, of two monkey cages. Brown had no idea what he was going to do with them. They had no functional purpose in his plans, unless you could call the tenderness of memory functional, and perhaps it is.

Miss Burke had strong loyal friends: the Rogers, George Cukor and Sam Goldwyn. It was Goldwyn — this man that some have pictured as interested only in amassing wealth, while others have derided his solecisms, perhaps making up his alleged slips of the tongue — who took Miss Burke's hand in his and said he would act as her agent and offered her a substantial amount of money a week, whether she was working or not. And it was Cukor who directed her in the art of talking movies, first in *A Bill of Divorcement,* then *Dinner at Eight,* and gave her the confidence that led to her many roles as what she has called "bird-witted ladies." So Miss Burke has carried on gallantly with humor, courage and understanding, but never with self-pity.

And what of Ziegfeld? Well, he had his years of renown and the era in which he earned it has long since passed away. I think he would say that life gave him a fair shake.

a gallery of
the glorified

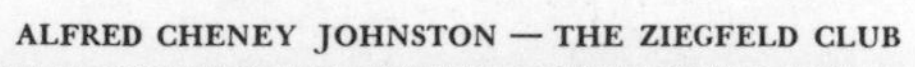

Frances White, star of the Midnight Frolics

ALFRED CHENEY JOHNSTON — THE ZIEGFELD CLUB

Vanda Hoff

ALFRED CHENEY JOHNSTON — THE ZIEGFELD CLUB

Kathryn Perry

THE ZIEGFELD CLUB

ALFRED CHENEY JOHNSTON — THE ZIEGFELD CLUB

Alta King

THE ZIEGFELD CLUB

Anastasia Reilly

ALFRED CHENEY JOHNSTON — THE ZIEGFELD CLUB

Ethel Hallor

THE ZIEGFELD CLUB

Helen Gates

Marie Wallace

THE ZIEGFELD CLUB

Bernice Ackerman

THE ZIEGFELD CLUB

Dorothy Leeds

THE ZIEGFELD CLUB

ALFRED CHENEY JOHNSTON — THE ZIEGFELD CLUB

Irene Marcellus

ALFRED CHENEY JOHNSTON — THE ZIEGFELD CLU

Julia Ross

Betty Martin

ALFRED CHENEY JOHNSTON — THE ZIEGFELD CLUB

Marie Shelton

THE ZIEGFELD CLUB

Martha Pierre

THE ZIEGFELD CLUB

THE ZIEGFELD CLU

Constance MacLaughlin

PICTURE COLLECTION, NEW YORK PUBLIC LIBRARY

PICTURE COLLECTION, NEW YORK PUBLIC LIBRARY

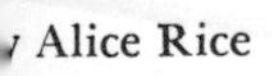

Alice Rice

Marie Stevens

Perle Germonde

THE ZIEGFELD CLUB

Scenes from the Follies of 1923

THE ZIEGFELD CLUB

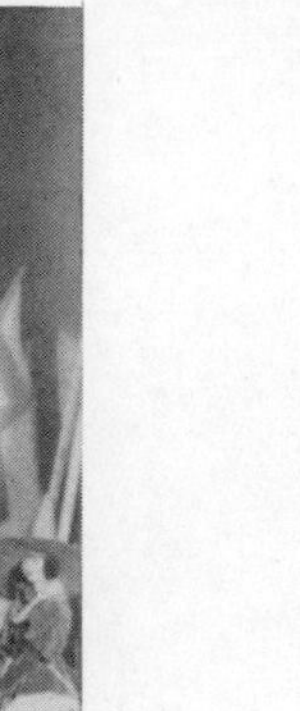

Scenes from the Follies of 1923

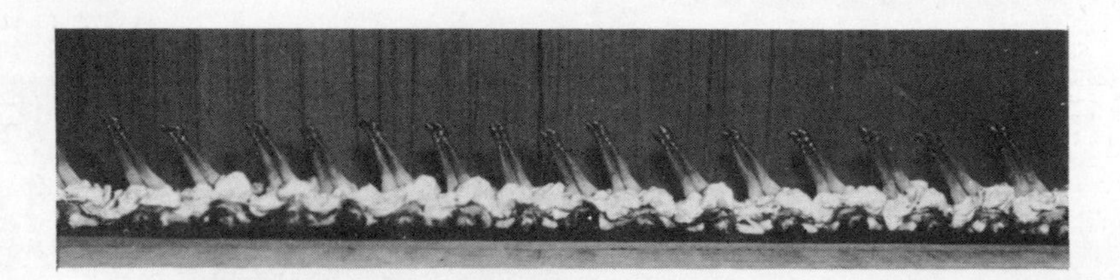

Ben Ali Haggin tableau
from Midnight Frolics – 1925

THE ZIEGFELD CLUB

THE ZIEGFELD CLUB

6

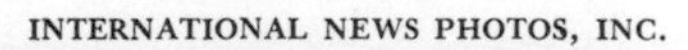

INTERNATIONAL NEWS PHOTOS, INC.

9

appendix

ZIEGFELD FOLLIES PRODUCTIONS: 1907-1931

YEAR	THEATRE	OPENING NIGHT	FEATURED PLAYERS
1907	Liberty	July 9, 1907	Nora Bayes
1908	New York Theatre Roof Garden	June 15, 1908	Nora Bayes Mae Murray William Powers
1909	New York Theatre Roof Garden	June 12, 1909	Mae Murray Eva Tanguay
1910	New York Theatre Roof Garden	June 20, 1910	George Bichel Fanny Brice Anna Held
1911	New York Theatre Roof Garden	June 26, 1911	Fanny Brice Dolly Sisters Leon Erroll Bert Williams
1912	Moulin Rouge	October 21, 1912	Leon Erroll Bert Williams
1913	New Amsterdam	June 16, 1913	Jose Collins Leon Erroll Ann Pennington Frank Tinney Nat M. Wills
1914	New Amsterdam	June 1, 1914	Leon Erroll Ann Pennington Bert Williams Ed Wynn
1915	New Amsterdam	June 21, 1915	Ina Claire Leon Erroll W. C. Fields Mae Murray Ann Pennington Bert Williams Ed Wynn
1916	New Amsterdam	June 12, 1916	Ina Claire Fanny Brice W. C. Fields Ann Pennington Frances White Bert Williams
1917	New Amsterdam	June 12, 1917	Fanny Brice Eddie Cantor W. C. Fields Peggy Hopkins Gus Minton Ann Pennington Lilyan Tashman Will Rogers

YEAR	THEATRE	OPENING NIGHT	FEATURED PLAYERS
1918	New Amsterdam	June 18, 1918	Eddie Cantor W. C. Fields Marilyn Miller Gus Minton Ann Pennington Will Rogers
1919	New Amsterdam	June 23, 1919	Eddie Cantor Ray & Johnny Dooley Eddie Dowling Marilyn Miller Van & Schenck Bert Williams
1920	New Amsterdam	June 22, 1920	Fanny Brice Ray Dooley Mary Eaton W. C. Fields Van & Schenck
1921	Globe	June 21, 1921	Fanny Brice Ray Dooley W. C. Fields Raymond Hitchcock Van & Schenck
1922	New Amsterdam	June 5, 1922	Gallagher & Shean Gilda Gray Will Rogers
1923	New Amsterdam	October 2, 1923	Fanny Brice Eddie Cantor Brooke Johns Ann Pennington
1924	New Amsterdam	June 24, 1924	Ann Pennington Will Rogers Vivienne Segal
1925	New Amsterdam	July 6, 1925	Ray Dooley W. C. Fields Clarence Nordstrom Ann Pennington Will Rogers Vivienne Segal Tiller Girls
1927	New Amsterdam	August 16, 1927	Eddie Cantor Irene Delroy Ruth Etting Dan Healy Albertina Rasche Girls
1931	Ziegfeld	July 1, 1931	Ruth Etting Helen Morgan Jack Pearl Harry Richman

index